Best pub walks
in south pembrokeshire

D1382622

Best Pub Walks

in

South

Pembrokeshire

Paul Williams

First published in 2008

© Text and Maps: Paul Williams
© Photographs: Paul Williams/Gwasg Carreg Gwalch

ISBN: 978-1-84524-082-0

Published by
Llygad Gwalch,
Ysgubor Plas, Llwyndyrys, Pwllheli, Gwynedd, Wales, LL53 6NG.
Tel: 01758 740432
e-mail: gai@llygadgwalch.com
www.llygadgwalch.com

contents

LOCATION MAP 8

INTRODUCTION 9
    Out and About 9
    Landscape and Culture 11
    History of the Pub... 27
    History of Inn Signs.. 30
    Place-names.. 32
    Tourist Information Centres 35
    The Country Code 36

THE WALKS
1. SAUNDERSFOOT TO WISEMAN'S BRIDGE AND AMROTH..................36
    Linear coastal and inland walk. 3.75 miles / 6 kilometres: Easy.
    The Royal Oak Inn, Saundersfoot;
    Wiseman's Bridge Inn; Amroth Arms.

2. PENALLY 44
    Coastal and inland walk. 4.5 miles / 7.25 kilometres: Moderate.
    The Cross Inn and Paddock Inn, Penally.

3. MANORBIER.. 51
    Coastal and inland walk. 6 miles / 9.5 kilometres: Moderate.
    Castle Inn, Manorbier.

4. STACKPOLE 58
    Coastal and inland walk. 6 miles / 9.5 kilometres: Moderate.
    The Stackpole Inn, Stackpole.

5. BOSHERSTON... 65
    Coastal and inland walk. 4 miles / 6.5 kilometres: Easy.
    St Govan's Country Inn, Bosherston.

6. ANGLE 72
    Coastal and inland walk. 3.75 miles / 6 kilometres: Easy.
    The Old Point House and Hibernia Inn, Angle.

7. CAREW AND MILTON... 79
    Inland walk. 2.2 miles / 3.5 kilometres: Easy.
    Carew Inn, Carew; Milton Brewery, Milton.

8. CRESSWELL QUAY... 86
    Riverside and inland walk. 5.5 miles / 8.75 kilometres: Moderate.
    Creselly Arms, Cresswell Quay.

9. LAWRENNY 92
    Riverside and inland walk. 3 miles / 4.75 kilometres: Easy.
    Lawrenny Arms, Lawrenny.

10. LANDSHIPPING 98
    Riverside and inland walk. 6 miles / 9.5 kilometres: Moderate.
    The Stanley Arms, Landshipping Ferry.

11. LAMPETER VALE (Llanddewi and Lampeter Velfrey)............... 105
    Inland walk. 6 miles / 9.5 kilometres: Moderate.
    Parc y Lan Inn, Llanddewi Velfrey.

12. HAVERFORDWEST... 113
    Riverside and inland walk. 5.5 miles / 8.75 kilometres: Easy.
    Bristol Trader, Haverfordwest.

13. BURTON TO LLANGWM.. 120
    Riverside walk. 4.75 miles / 7.5 kilometres: Easy.
    Jolly Sailor, Burton Ferry; Stable Bar, Burton;
    The Cottage, Llangwm.

14. ST ISHMAEL'S AND SANDY HAVEN... 128
    Coastal and inland walk. 5.25 miles / 8.5 kilometres: Moderate.
    The Brook Inn, St Ishmael's.

15. DALE... 134
    Coastal walk. 7 miles / 11 kilometres: Moderate.
    Griffin Inn, Dale.

16. MARLOES.. 143
    Coastal walk. 7 miles / 11 kilometres: Moderate.
    Lobster Pot Inn, Marloes.

17. LITTLE HAVEN 149
    Coastal and inland walk. 3.25 miles / 5 kilometres: Easy.
    The Castle, St Bride's Inn and the Swan Inn, Little Haven.

18. NOLTON HAVEN 154
    Coastal and inland walk. 3.6 miles / 5.75 kilometres: Easy.
    Mariners' Inn, Nolton Haven.

FEATURES
    Of Gerald of Wales and Welsh Hospitality 54
    Landsker 107

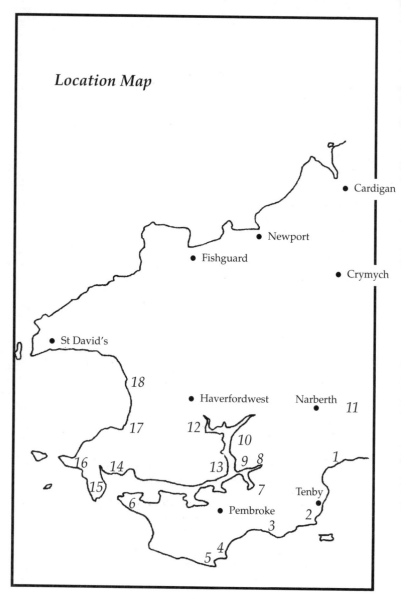

Location Map

Cardigan

Newport

Fishguard

Crymych

St David's

18

Haverfordwest

Narberth

11

17

12

10

16

14

13

9   8

15

7

Tenby

6

1

Pembroke

2

3

4

5

Introduction

Out and About

Those familiar with my *Circular Walks in South Pembrokeshire* will find thirteen new walks in this volume, however the five old favourites are well worth repeating! All walks are easy to follow, and clear directions are given. The exact location for the starting point of each walk is noted, and how to get there. Relevant bus routes and numbers are included – though given that Pembrokeshire is a rural area services can be infrequent. Nor do all buses operate on Sundays. Train services are also listed. Check with Information Centres for full details. The County Council with contributions from the National Park operate summer Coastal bus services to the more popular coastal areas, and their popularity has led to the majority continuing to operate through the winter months. There is adequate parking space at the start of each walk – precise details are given.

Walks vary in length from 2.2 miles/3.5 kilometres to 7 miles/11 kilometres. The routes utilise the long distance Pembrokeshire Coast Path, public footpaths, bridleways and the occasional permissive path, as at Lawrenny and Landshipping. They are well maintained, and clearly signposted and waymarked – a yellow arrow or waymark indicating a public footpath, a blue one a bridleway. The National Park is in the process of replacing as many stiles as praticable with gates, making access for the less able easier. An acorn indicates the route is a long distance path, and is often confused with the, quite separate, National Trust's logo of an oak leaf. Many people are uncertain of how long a walk of, for example, 7 miles would take. As a rough guide an average walker would expect to cover 3 miles/4.75 kilometres an hour over level ground, on the ascent an hour for every 2000 feet/600 metres. Sketch maps for each walk are provided – but the author advises that the local Ordnance Survey (OS) 1:25, 000 series are used alongside these.

The 1:50 000 series (1.25 inches = 1 mile/2 centimetres = 1 kilometre) cover the county in three maps: Cardigan, St David's and Haverfordwest, and Tenby. Those preferring greater detail will wish to acquire the yellow covered Outdoor Leisure 1:25 000 series (2.5 inches = 1 mile/4 centimetres = 1 kilometre). The series cover the county in two maps: 35 North Pembrokeshire and 36 South Pembrokeshire. All walks in this guide will be found on the 36 South Pembrokeshire map. Much has been said of the recent "right to roam", the Right of Access on foot to large areas of Wales given by the introduction in 2005 of the Countryside and Rights of Way Act. In practice this means a right to walk on open county ie moor, mountain, heath and down, and on registered common land. This "Access Land" (see OS maps) makes up about 10% of the National Park, largely in the north of the county. It does not apply to built up areas, farmyards, field and woodland, where public paths only can be utilised.

The grading system used is largely self-explanatory. Easy walks involve short walks over easy terrain, with little variation in contour. Moderate may have one or two short steep sections, with a little more variety in landscape. The author stresses however that the term 'easy' and 'moderate' are used by comparison to 'challenging' and 'strenuous' – all walks can have their problems and please heed the notice on page 35. History notes are included which are designed to give both an historical note of the pubs featured on the walk, as well as a quick snapshot of the particular area, what gives a place in landscape or historical terms it's own brand of uniqueness. Many Pembrokeshire pubs close in the afternoons, so check opening times if required; phone numbers of all pubs are listed. All provide food, and many welcome children, and will allow dogs. Some offer accommodation. As all but two of the walks are circular they may be joined at any convenient point, (or either end in the case of the linear ones!), and details of parking at the most accessible points are listed under a number of the walks. Included under facilities are the nearest BT telephones, public toilets, cafes, Post Offices and shops, youth hostels, caravan sites etc. Most small towns and many farms will offer B&B – check with Information Centres if you are interested. Also listed under facilities are any additional places of interest in the neighbourhood, for example gardens and garden centres.

Finally a word of warning. Footpaths get muddy, the foreshore can get slippery, and cliffs can be dangerous. Take care! Ensure you have adequate clothing, and the proper footwear, ie boots or stout shoes, for each walk. Follow the Country Code!

lanscape ano culture

Pembrokeshire – the name is an Anglicisation of the Welsh *Pen Fro*, or Land's End – juts out into the sea at the south west corner of Wales. Surrounded on three sides by the powerhouses of the Atlantic Ocean and the Irish Sea it's spectacular cliffs are studded with glittering coves and bays. One of the essential features of the landscape is it's many isolated peninsulas; another the extraordinary flatness of the land. Only the heather clad hills of the Preselis (home of the bluestones of Stonehenge), the great stone outcrops at Strumble Head, St David's and Treffgarne gorge, and the southern Ridgeway, rise above the uniformity. In the south, like a sword slash, the Milford Haven tears the plateau apart. The county is renowned for it's magnificent coast and it's sandy shores, yet it has a magic and uniqueness which goes beyond these, for it is a microcosm of the major habitats to be found in

Skomer Island puffins

Britain. The coastal waters are particularly rich in marine flora and fauna; a substantial part of Pembrokeshire's coastline, the shore, seabed and sea surrounding her islands, and the Milford Haven waterway, being designated as the Pembrokeshire Marine Special Area of Conservation (SAC) in December 2004. The coast plays host to some five thousand grey seals; harbour porpoises and bottlenose dolphins are common sitings. The bird islands of Grassholm, Skomer and Skokholm are of international importance. Grassholm is one of the world's largest gannetries, Skomer probably the planet's top spot for the Manx shearwater. Home to razorbills and guillemots, fulmars, kittiwakes and puffins the islands are not to be missed. Good mainland locations for birdwatchers are, in the north of the county, at Dinas island and Strumble Head, and, in the south, near Bosherston, at Stack Rocks and Stackpole Head.

Pembrokeshire's cliffs, at their highest in the north, are regal in spring and early summer. Magical yellows of gorse and bird's-foot trefoil mingle with the pinks of the thrift and the whites of sea campion. The succession of flowers continues, as if to an ordered floral banquet, from March to August. In the south are the main sand dune systems, extensive at Penally and Freshwater West, with smaller systems at Broad Haven South and Manorbier. Northern systems, some protected, are at Whitesands Bay, Newport and Poppit Sands. Sheltered behind shingle banks or sand bars are pockets of saltmarsh. Usually found at the mouths of estuaries they are hostile to all but the most salt tolerant plants. The Gann, at Pickleridge near Dale, is perhaps the most important, with others at Newport and the Teifi at Cardigan. Together with intertidal mudflats, formed by the accumulation of silt where fresh and salt waters meet, they are highly important feeding grounds for thousands of overwintering waders and wildfowl. The mudflats of Angle Bay, and the western and eastern arms of the Cleddau river, are particularly popular.

Freshwater habitats include the marshes found at the flood

plains of rivers and streams. Good examples are at Penally, and at Pentood marsh in Cilgerran Wildlife Centre. The largest area of open water in the National Park are the delightful lily ponds at Bosherston, a highly popular summer venue. Llys y Frân Reservoir and Country Park, opened in the 1970s, attracts a number of winter waterfowl, as well as offering water sports and fishing. Remnants of the oak forest which once covered Pembrokeshire remain. Clinging to the sides of isolated valleys and hills, and along the steeper sections of rivers, they have a unique beauty and atmosphere. The Gwaun valley in it's summer yellows and greens, or with the early morning winter mist rising from the water, is rightly famous, whilst hidden amongst the steep oak woods of the Cleddau are Norman river castles; whitewashed Benton opposite Lawrenny, or Carew, glimpsed through the trees bordering the Carew river. Less dramatic are the uniform stands of coniferous plantations which dot the uplands.

In the north of the county are the Preseli hills, extensive areas of lowland heath, acid grassland and moorland. They are predominantly heath, dominated by heather, with gorse in western areas giving way to bilberry in the east. Patches of wet heath or bogland, with sphagnum and cotton grass, break up the landscape. Smaller areas of low lying heath are at Strumble Head and St David's Head. Roadside verges, and traditional hedgebanks, whether of stone and/or turf, are ablaze with the colours of wild flowers in spring and early summer. The semi-natural specialised grassland of farms have less to offer in terms of wildlife, though many have areas of waste ground, or a pond. In the south the limestone cliffs and plateau, with it's short springy turf and superb maritime flora, is one of the most impressive limestone areas in Britain.

Geologically Pembrokeshire is of spectacular interest. Not only does it offer magnificently exposed rock formations around it's coast, but the series of rocks on display range in an unbroken series from the very oldest Pre-Cambrian, from 3,000 million years ago, to the Carboniferous coal measures of 300 million years ago. The Pre-Cambrian rocks, formed before the appearance of any obvious fossilized life, occur in a small area extending from Whitesands Bay to Porth Llysgi. Later Lower Palaeozoic rocks, the Cambrian, Ordovician and Silurian systems which begin 570 million years ago, occur, like the Pre-Cambrian, in the north of the county. These igneous and sedimentary rocks were faulted and folded at the end of the Silurian period, some 400 million years ago, during the great Caledonian earth movements. As a result a WSW – ENE grain was imposed across the north of the county; one further result being the formation of St David's peninsula.

By contrast the rocks in south Pembrokeshire are mainly Upper Palaeozoic. Devonian Old Red Sandstone covers most of the north side of Milford Haven, Dale and Angle peninsulas, and part of Caldey Island, while a superb limestone section runs from Linney Head to Stackpole Head, with further sections at Lydstep and Giltar Point at Penally. A significant coal measure runs across the county from Saundersfoot to St Brides Bay. After the depositions of the coal measures the land was again subject to massive earth movements, this time the Armorican orogeny of 290 million years ago. However now a WNW – ESE grain was imposed across the south of the county.

The present flatness of the land is due to constant wave erosion at a time when the sea covered the landscape, probably during the late Tertiary period some 17,000 million years ago. Only the more resistant igneous outcrops, like Carn Llidi and Garn Fawr, remained as islands above the sea. Recent evidence suggests that Britain's status as an island dates to some time between 450,000 and 200,000 years ago when the natural land dam between the Strait of Dover and France was destroyed in a megaflood, with a wall of water forced through it with at least ten times the force of the Boxing Day tsunami of 2004. There had been human occupation in Britain by Homo Heidelbergensis and Neanderthal man from 700,000 years ago, but between

180,000 and 60,000 years ago all evidence of occupation dies out. Even during glaciation and low sea levels the newly formed Channel river seems to have acted as a barrier to further human occupation until some 60,000 years ago when sea levels fell to a low enough level for crossing.

On at least two occasions Pembrokeshire lay under the Irish Sea glacier; the first occasion, some 120,000 years ago, covered the entire county, while the second, 20,000 to 17,000 years ago, affected only the north. Before the advent of this last ice sheet drove him south Palaeolithic man, Old Stone Age man, had made his appearance, living in caves on Caldey island and at Hoyle's Mouth near Penally. 15,000 years ago the climate became gradually warmer, the land was re-colonised, and with the melting of the ice under the glacier deep and narrow gorges, originally formed with the initial retreat of the glacier, were further deepened as the meltwater scythed it's way to the sea. The Gwaun valley is the most impressive example of a meltwater channel in Britain. With the final melting of the ice, and the rise in sea levels some 10,000 years ago, the existing river valleys of Milford Haven and Solva were drowned by the incoming tides, assuming their present shape, and the forests were gradually submerged to remain exposed at coastal beaches, as at Whitesands Bay and Amroth, at low tides.

Mesolithic culture began to develop in the county some 10,000 years ago, with Mesolithic man continuing to live, much as his ancestor Palaeolithic man had done, by hunting and fishing, with perhaps a little primitive farming, and some movement to open settlement in flimsy shelters. However it was a change in the use of stone tools that marked one cultural difference – there have been finds of his flint tools at Nab Head near St Brides Haven, Swanlake Bay near Manorbier, and on Caldey island. Much of the marshy wooded lowlands where he hunted gradually fell under the encroaching sea – perhaps the tales of great floods, lost cities, and the fine towns of Cantref Y Gwaelod (the Low Hundred) are folk memories of these drowned lands.

This Mesolithic hunter-gatherer society gradually gave way some 6,000 years ago to the Neolithic era. With the Neolithic age came a new relationship with the land; the given environment was modified to include domesticated wheat and barley, sheep, cattle and goats. This meant the clearance of the woodland and fixed settlement, a settled home in the natural landscape of the Mesolithic era. It has long been heralded that this Neolithic farming revolution was introduced into Wales, as Britain, by incomers, with the Mesolithic inhabitants forced into the margins, but perhaps it was a more a mixture of the migration of ideas and settlers that forged the new society. Of their day to day settlements, made of wood (only in the Orkneys at the tip of Scotland did the climate require stone) little survives – there is a single trace at Clegyr Boia, near St David's. However the landscape they inhabited is marked by ritual reminders of their presence, the great stone burial chambers. Perhaps with kinship with the land came the need to express that kinship through ritual possession of the landscape through reminders of their ancestors – longevity of kin given expression in stone and earth, the symbol of territory and ownership of landscape. There are fine examples of their burial chambers at Pentre Ifan near Nevern, one of the finest in Britain, with others, plentiful along the north coast and on the Preselis, rarer in the south.

It has been argued that the late Neolithic/early Bronze Age eras heralded the development of a new ideology and society associated with the rising and setting sun and moon. There was a deterioration in climate, with a volcanic explosion in Iceland blotting out the sun, resulting in freezing weather and perpetual rain, along with famine and crop failures. There was a new emphasis on the way of the heavens. Along with the decline in monumental burial chambers – they were replaced by single round burial chambers built on higher and more visible ground than their predecessors, as at Foel Drygarn in the Preselis, went the building of stone circles, henges and stone alignments; these processional alignments could be interpreted as processional journeys from death to the afterlife. There is a fine stone circle at Gors Fawr, near Mynachlog Ddu in the Preseli hills. There seems to have been a desertion of settlements and a re-establishment of cleared woodland, though the agricultural system appears to have remained stable. It is believed that the arrival of the Bronze Age (2,000 to 600 BC) was heralded by the immigration of the Beaker people from Europe (so called because of their characteristic decorated pottery drinking vessels), carrying knowledge of copper and bronze, and it's use in weaponry and jewellery, but again as with the Neolithic, it may have been as much a movement of ideas and trade.

The late Bronze Age witnessed a further deterioration in climate and widespread movements of population in Europe. Upland areas were abandoned, and for the first time pressure on farmland resulted in the building of defensive settlements. Strategic sites favoured were coastal headlands and hilltops; this pattern continued with the gradual development of iron working, and as the Iron Age progresses society takes on a more aggressive face – the larger forts perhaps exercising some control over the smaller defended settlements with regional grouping forming the basis of future tribal areas. The Deer Park fort by Marloes makes full use of it's coastal setting and natural defensive position, likewise the inland forts of Foel Drygarn (superimposed on the Bronze Age burial site) and Carn Ingli by Newport. Castell Henllys, near Nevern, is a superb re-creation of an Iron Age settlement, and well worth a visit. One long standing theory has it that it was at the beginning of the Iron Age that the Celts arrived in numbers in Britain, speaking the ancestors of the modern Celtic languages, however there is no evidence to suggest any major influx of people. The so called "Celtic" languages may date back to the late Neolithic/early Bronze Age, if not earlier; how and when they arrived in Britain is not known. Society as it developed would have come under the influence of the "Celtic" mores of Iron Age Europe – the only real Celts at the time were the continental Gauls, though Classical commentators had begun to refer to these Iron Age European peoples as Celts from 500 BC onwards.

The Roman period begins with Julius Caesar's landing on the Kent coastline in 55 BC, however Romanisation of the country proper begins with the invasion of Claudius in AD 43 – by AD 78 the conquest of Wales was complete. Existing tribal groupings in the south of Wales were the Silures of the south-east, with, to the west, the Demetae. The conquest of the Demetae seems to have been quick and efficient, and whilst there is little evidence of Roman settlement west of the fort at Carmarthen recent finds of a substantial villa near Wolf's Castle, and traces of a road leading from Carmarthen towards Haverfordwest suggest Roman influence may be greater than once thought. With the collapse of Roman rule in the early 5th century the pattern of small scale farming continued, much as it had done during the Iron Age, with services and obligations owed by smaller farmers and bondsmen to the "nobles". However the removal of a central authority left the land open to raids, first by the Irish – an Irish dynasty was most probably in power in west Wales by the end of the 5th century – and later by the Vikings, who in addition to destroying many settlements, including St David's monastic settlement on several occasions, gave their own names to many of the more prominent landmarks; Grassholm, Skokholm and Solva all have Norse connections.

The 5th and 6th centuries was the Age of the Saints, when peregrini, travelling monks from Europe and Ireland, helped consolidate the hold of Christianity in Wales and lay the foundations of the Celtic church. Central to the local community was the llan, so common a feature of Welsh place-names, and being an enclosure, often circular (and often making use of an already circular site) for burial. Manorbier's churchyard is of this type. Other early Christian evidence derives from the many Christian stones, inscribed with the names of the aristocracy, and marking the site of their graves. Some of the earliest are in Latin and/or ogham – ogham an Irish script of cut notches along the edge of the stone to indicate spelling, an indication of early Irish presence in the area. There is a fine example in Cilgerran's churchyard. Ogham had ceased by 600, later stones being in Latin. More elaborate stones, decorated with linework and fine crosses, may have marked church property. There are two decorated 10th to 11th century crosses in Penally church, which may have been carved for a monastic settlement in the vicinity.

One pioneer of the new church was St David, who established his monastic settlement in the St David's area – his original monastery may have been at Whitesands Bay, rather than on the site of the present cathedral. The community's way of life was based on worship and hard manual labour. No oxen were used in ploughing, the yoke was put to their own shoulders, and once labour was completed time was given to contemplation. Diet was vegetarian, based on bread and herbs, and, probably, water, though what was their main type of drink is uncertain. With the new monasticism came a new mysticism and asceticism. Ascetics chose solitary places to reside, often living in clochan – beehive shaped buildings made of local stone. There is at Pwll Deri near Strumble Head, in Tal y Gaer farmyard, a building which may well have been a clochan of this type. Pembrokeshire's islands, beaches and coves offered further opportunities for the solitary; St Govan's near Bosherston, with it's chapel in a cleft of rock, is one of the best known – the ocean for these ascetics often replaced the desert of the Egyptian

St. Govan's Chapel

fathers. The Age of the Saints was also the heroic age of Britain, the age of Arthur, defender of civilisation after the Roman collapse to barbarism. The 11th and 12th century Welsh tales of the Mabinogion relate some of the earliest tales of Arthur in literature; Culwch and Olwen telling of Arthur and his knights' hunt of a magical boar across St David's peninsula, the Nyfer valley and the Preseli hills.

The years 400 to 600 were crucial to the formation of Wales as a country, as it was to the Scottish and English nations, and it is the fortunes of the early kingdoms and their rulers that give the period the political flavour of the age. By the mid 10th century it was possible, if only temporarily, for Hywel Dda (the Good) to have added the kingdom of Deheubarth (Cardiganshire, Pembrokeshire, Carmarthenshire and Gower) to the northern and eastern kingdoms of Gwynedd and Powys, and to have consolidated the Law of Wales, quite possibly at a meeting held at Whitland in west Carmarthenshire. However by the late 11th century a new and feared power was in the land.

The Norman conquest of 1066 was to change the face of Wales, as it had done England's. The occupation of England had already traumatised existing society, and the conduct of the campaign had led to comment on the ensuing *sacrifice of human life* by Pope Gregory VII in 1080, ally to William I; in the expeditions of 1069-70 in the north of England the surviving population had been left to starvation and cannibalism. Initially Rhys ap Tewdwr managed to retain his rule over Deheubarth, though acknowledging overlordship to William who crossed his lands in 1081 on a "pilgrimage" to St David's – no doubt he also visited Whitesands Bay, the normal embarkation point for Ireland, and a possible embarkation point for any invasion of Ireland. However after Rhys' death a series of lordships were established in this south-western corner of the Marches of Wales. Moving from his base on the Severn, Roger, Earl of Shrewsbury, crossed into Pembrokeshire by way of Cardiganshire, his son establishing the Lordship of Pembroke.

Castles were built at Roch in the west, and Wiston, Llawhaden, Narberth and Amroth on Carmarthen Bay – with isolated Norman settlements in the north at Newport and Cilgerran. For a time an almost definable frontier stretched across

Pembroke Castle

the centre of the county – a convenient dividing line later termed the Landsker (poss. Norse for frontier) by later historians. Early castles were earth and timber, either ringwork, or motte and bailey, and sited not only on strategic high points, but also close to the rivers and sea-lanes. With consolidation of power and the continuing need for defence stone was used – Pembroke one of the finest and most impregnable, and consequently one of the few never to be occupied by the Welsh, who continued to oppose Norman settlement by force of arms.

South Pembrokeshire formed part of the Marches of Wales, a region where taxes and law were the prerogatives of the lords in the castle. The new colony was organised on the English pattern, the first such in Wales, and had, by at least 1138, independent "palatine" status. This is the basis of Pembrokeshire's claim to be the premier county of Wales. Prior to the Norman arrival villages had been the largest settlements; with colonisation came the development of Anglo-Norman towns, with Pembroke the first county town west of the Severn. The local population was absorbed into the growing Norman colony, supplemented by English, Irish and Flemish settlers. To the north the Welsh maintained their way of life, and their own language; in the castles the new lords planned the consolidation of their power through the language of French.

Until the Edwardian conquest of Wales in 1282 Wales outside

the Marches – *pura Wallia* (pure or non Norman Wales) – was allowed to retain it's separate identity. Pre-eminent amongst the Welsh princes of the 12th century was the Lord Rhys, Rhys ap Gruffydd. He ruled from the Welsh stronghold of Deheubarth at Dinefwr castle in Carmarthenshire, which may be his work. It was a time of stability for Welsh culture; he hosted the first eisteddfod at Cardigan castle in 1176, with competitors arriving from abroad as well as other parts of Wales. He founded an abbey at Nevern, and rebuilt Cardigan castle. After his death Llywelyn the Great held sway; however with his death in 1282, and the end of the Welsh drive for independence, (until the Owain Glyndŵr uprising in the early 15th century), the Welsh princes ruled under a watchful English eye. To serve the lords in the castle traders and craftsmen settled close by, and in time these communities were granted trade rights and privileges, and later charters confirming borough status. This pattern of urban growth, imitated by the Welsh princes, formed the basis of the urban structure of Wales until the Industrial Revolution.

Norman society was nothing if not rigid; at the head of it's structure was God, with the King and villein all bound to those above by duty. The expression of that social order was in land, the great estates of the Norman lords, and the obligations of their feudal tenants. The most fertile land was given to their followers, the Welsh were forced to the uplands where they were allowed to keep their customs and law, whilst in the new urban areas settlement was restricted, at least initially, to the non Welsh. Of the medieval strip field system there are survivals at Angle. Inevitably the Normans found the Celtic church too independent and outdated, and it was quickly remodelled along Continental lines. St David's became one of four Welsh dioceses, with outlying churches organised into a parish system; new churches with defensive towers being built on the old llanau, and the dedications to Celtic saints usually being removed and rededicated to Roman ones. Celtic monasticism was also tied to Europe and European orders – a new Cistercian monastery was established at Whitland in 1140. At no time was St David's ever garrisoned, though an episcopal system was imposed, and, circa 1182, work began on a new cathedral.

It may be possible that the asceticism that was contemporary with St David and his followers continued through the centuries; certainly there is evidence for ascetic practice during the 11th and early 12th centuries. The Age of the Saints provided plenty of legends and holy sites for an aspiring ascetic, and for the growing number of pilgrims to St David's hospitals were built by Norman bishops at Llawhaden and Whitewell at St David's, with sister's houses at Minwear on the eastern Cledddau, and possibly at Angle. Abbeys, priories and chapels were built, as at St Dogmaels, Haverfordwest and St Non's. The Knights Hospitallers of St John of Jerusalem had their Welsh headquarters at Slebech, on the opposite side of the river to Minwear, where they administered to the sick and recruited for the Crusades. Yet for all their piety there was a dark side to the Norman vision. The Celtic vision had been one of nature mysticism and humanity, the Normans introduced savage visions of heaven and hell.

By the time of the accession to the English throne in 1485 of Henry VII, born in Pembroke castle, society in the Marches and in Wales as a whole had become more peaceful and orderly. Castles could be modified to become comfortable manor houses, as at Carew, and the Welsh gentry who had leant their support to Henry Tudor as he had taken to the field against Richard III at Bosworth were suitably rewarded. There was greater opportunity for social mobility in society as a whole, and the growth of

Carew Castle

urban life, the most marked effect of the Norman conquest, continued. The Acts of Union of 1536-43 marked the political merger of Wales with England. The power of the Norman Lords and their independence was ended and Pembrokeshire was made a county, with, for the first time, much the same boundaries as now, and the dissolution of the monasteries ended the power of the abbeys. Pilgrimages were now seen as idolaterous. A new faith was in the land, and all power was under the control of the king, Henry VIII.

In the centuries that followed life came to be dominated by the demands of agriculture and trade, and the years from the Acts of Union to 1770 have been characterised as the age of the gentry, of the rise of the yeoman farmer. It was they who received the bulk of economic surplus and who exercised control over the destiny of their fellow men. The Acts of Union had abolished the privileges of the Marches of Wales tying the fortunes of their lords to those of Henry VIII's state. The dissolution of the monasteries in 1540 similarly asserted the authority of the Tudor state. Following the break with Rome the Church of England was established, but it is open to debate how wholeheartedly the new church was adopted. In the towns those that had access to the sea grew into flourishing ports, and every small creek and cove seemed to have it's own sloop, often locally built. Out went wool, cattle and grain, and in came general merchandise, wine and spices, not to mention the often highly profitable smuggled cargo. The Civil War of the mid 17th century raised tensions and politics between neighbours – the Welsh mainly favoured the king, while the south were, usually, for Parliament – but if politics were uncertain and allegiances inconstant the underlying economy remained stable. It was during the Civil War that the castles saw their last moments of glory; however any which had served the Royalist cause were quickly rendered defenceless by Cromwell after victory. Many were left to fade into obscurity, to find uses in later centuries as Romantic ruins.

The 19th century had as profound effect on Pembrokeshire as had the arrival of the Normans. The coming of the railways in mid and late century heralded new communication and commercial advantages. Visitors began to arrive in increasing numbers at resort towns such as Tenby and Manorbier, already growing in importance during the late 18th century. Three new towns were established on the shores around Milford Haven. Neyland, previously a small fishing village, was planned by Brunel as the terminus of his South Wales railway, and as the terminus of Irish and transatlantic steamships – the latter functions transferring to Fishguard in the late 1900s. Milford Haven was laid out as a private initiative in 1793; among the earliest settlers a group of Quaker whalers from Nantucket. By 1900 to 1914 the town had risen to become one of the busiest fishing ports in the country. Across the water Pembroke Dock grew with the Admiralty dockyard established there in 1814 – for much of the century it was the world's most advanced shipyard, with revolutionary warships and five royal yachts to it's credit. Admiralty presence in the town finally ended in 2008 with the demise of the Royal Maritime Auxiliary Service.

There were many local industrial concerns. Coal mining had always been of importance, production reaching it's peak during the late 18th and early 19th centuries at sites on St Brides Bay, at the confluence of the eastern and western Cleddau, and in the Saundersfoot and Kilgetty area. To exploit the latter's many pits the Saundersfoot Railway and Harbour Company was formed in 1829, and nearby, in Pleasant Valley, the Stepaside Ironworks flourished from 1849 to 1877. Whole villages were given over to quarrying, as at Cilgerran, and at Porthgain and Abereiddi where slates and bricks were also produced. Many of these concerns were comparatively shortlived, and had ceased operating by early or mid 20th century; Hook, on the western Cleddau, was the last colliery, closing in 1949, Porthgain's industrial age ended in 1931, and the Saundersfoot Railway and Harbour Company rail lines were raised by the 1940s. There were changes in agriculture too, cheap fertilizers raised yields and meant the end of the centuries old lime burning industry; cheap imported grain milled in larger town mills meant the end of local flour and feed producing mills, and cheap metals spelt the end of the local smithy. The revolution in land transport meant the end of the coastal trade, and local shipbuilding.

Politically the introduction of county councils in the late 1880s, with elected officials, replaced the centuries rule by the squierarchy, the local landowners who on a voluntary basis had occupied the leading positions in the county. The 19th century was also the hey-day of non conformism, active since the 17th century. Chapels, built out of subscriptions raised by local congregations, began to appear in ever increasing numbers in the towns and villages, particularly in the Welsh speaking areas. Indeed as public buildings the chapels are more truly the Welsh vernacular architecture than the great Norman castles. It was also the age of the restoration of the existing Norman and Celtic churches. Since the Reformation there had been little new church building, and existing churches had been either barely maintained or allowed to decay. Old ones were renovated, and new ones, with inventive variations on existing styles, were built, as at Capel Colman in the north east of the county near Boncath.

By the mid 20th century modernisation had transformed the county. 1960 saw the first oil port, Esso, established. Though Esso closed in 1983 Milford Haven's claim to be a leading energy port has been boosted by the arrival of two new Liquid Natural Gas (LNG) import and storage facilities in the shape of South Hook LNG, and the smaller Dragon LNG, which together with Texaco and Murco oil refineries form the major part of the energy portfolio. The energy industry, agriculture and tourism, the public services and the small business sector are now the backbones of the local economy. Pembrokeshire was designated Britain's first coastal National Park in 1952, and the long distance Coast Path was opened in 1970. Pembrokeshire returned as a county in it's own right in April 1996, having been from 1974 part of the larger county of Dyfed – the National Park was similarly made a separate authority.

history of the pub

It is thought the first inns date back to Roman times, when inns and the smaller *tavernae*, or taverns, were established alongside the newly built roads for officials and other travellers. Alcohol served was largely wine, imported from the empire, though ale brewed from cereals may also have been served; almost certainly the secrets of brewing were known in Britain by the Neolithic period. The later Saxons continued the tradition of the tavern, each village having houses where court could be held, and ale drunk. By the time the Normans had established power the creation of towns in the shadow of the castles included the establishment of permanent ale houses sited often close by the market square and church. They reintroduced wine, and popularised the drinking of cider, however ale remained the drink of choice. In Pembrokeshire, with the growth of St David's as a shrine, inns were opened to provide for pilgrims and travellers – Pope Calixtus II equated two pilgrimages to St David's with one to Rome; it was also said that three was the equal of one to Jerusalem.

There was a strong link between the monasteries and the brewing industry, the monasteries creating guest houses and hospices, often offering free bread and ale. Guests however were usually restricted to the upper classes and pilgrims, the middle and lower classes staying in inns. Though definitions were to later become blurred an inn provided rooms, the tavern food and drink, while the humble ale house served only ale. Whilst monks were well known as brewers, funds for the monastery raised by sale, it was traditionally, as with the baking of bread, women's work, excess being sold on. Regulation of the trade came early on, with the Magna Carta including a decree to standardise the measure for corn, wine and ale – the latter the origins of the measure of a pint.

One major revolution in drinking habits was the 15th century introduction of hops from Europe, where they had been in use from the 8th century. The result was the introduction of a new drink – beer. Ale remained the first choice for a long time since it was untainted by the preservative hop flower, beer giving a sharper flavour, whilst ale was stronger and sweeter; prior to introduction of the hop ale had been flavoured with herbs like rosemary. However beer had better keeping properties, and by the mid 16th century Dutch and Flemish immigrants had well established hop gardens in Kent and Sussex. With the dissolution of the monasteries by Henry VIII from 1538 onwards the pattern of accommodation inevitably changed, wealthy travellers now seeking the shelter of the more substantial town inns that began to develop, with reasonable rooms, food and stabling on offer.

By the 18th century public houses were being purpose built, offering several rooms for different classes of drinkers, but without however offering accommodation. Many ale houses, often one room affairs, upgraded, others continuing their trade serving the lower classes. The improvements in the road network and of the horse drawn coach transformed many of the existing inns into coaching inns, with the better town inns adding function rooms to their business portfolio. The development of seaside resorts like Tenby encouraged similar expansion. Further developments saw the beginnings of the tied house, the brewer making deliveries to particular pubs in his area, and the brewer's dray – the low heavy horse cart used for haulage – became a familiar sight in the towns.

Drinking habits had seen a large increase in brandy and gin consumption since the late 17th century onwards, and there had been a number of acts introduced to curb the habit and turn the taste back to beer, seen as more wholesome, water being boiled as part of the brewing process. Part of the problem had been the exemption of spirits from duty, whilst it remained payable on beer. The introduction of the 1830 Beer Act sought to curb spirit consumption and promote agriculture and beer by abolishing the beer duty and introducing the beer shop, or beer house. For the small sum of two guineas any householder could obtain a beer licence to sell beer and cider only, the public houses retaining the right to sell also spirits and wine. The result was thousands of new beer houses, with many tradesmen adding the sale of beer as a sideline. However the beer shops were often poorly run, leading to outbreaks of drunken behaviour. They soon became known as Tom and Jerry shops, so named after two Regency bucks from Tom Egan's 1821 comic serial *Life In London*, featuring the often disreputable adventures of Corinthian Tom and his country cousin Jerry Hawthorne – the original Tom and Jerry.

Alongside the rise in Tom and Jerry shops went the rise in the Temperance movement. Organised in 1828 the movement had favoured the development of the beer shop, some members quite happy to recommend beer and wine when drunk in moderation. However moves were afoot to curb Sunday opening hours, and by mid century ways were sought to curb the numbers of beer houses altogether. The 1869 Wine and Beer House Act gave control of all licensed premises to the magistrate; with the result that many smaller premises closed, and with little possibility of new ones opening the larger brewers began to extend their control – the introduction of refrigeration in the 1880s further helped industrialisation. 1881 saw the introduction of the Welsh Sunday Closing Act. Each movement of religious revival in Wales was accompanied by temperance promotion, many local landowners in Pembrokeshire, notably at Stackpole and Lawrenny, lending their support by outlawing pubs on their estates. By 1914 and the Defence of the Realm Act even tighter laws were introduced, it became illegal to buy anyone a drink, even your mate, the practice of treating seen as encouraging excessive drinking. A culture of excessive drinking among servicemen and munitions workers was a great fear, drink being identified as being as much the enemy as Germany in certain political quarters.

By the 1930s attitudes to the pub, to drinking, and to temperance were changing. Pubs were coming to be seen as social centres, rather than as a centre for drunkenness, and calls for a return to the restrictions of the Great War were rejected. The post 1945 growth of tourism favoured the development of the pub, and 1961 saw the introduction of the Licensing Act giving the choice to counties to reject Sunday closing. Pembrokeshire went wet in 1968. The 1960s and 1970s witnessed a trend towards extension of existing pubs in tourist areas, with some new ones opening as with the Lawrenny Arms, and with refurbishment of others, though with hindsight the 1970s idea of style was not always of the best. Others resisted and retain their original character. One other major change of recent years has been the growth in favour of keg beers, the 1960s consolidation of the brewing industry led to the closure of many small brewers, and the move to develop a stable beer with a longer shelf life. Unlike real ale, which undergoes a secondary fermentation normally in the pub cellar, keg beer has been pasteurised, thus killing off the beer bacteria that causes fermentation by heating – CO_2 being then added. One response to this was the formation of the Campaign for Real Ale, CAMRA, in 1971. Another recent change was the implementation of the Licensing Act of 2003, which transferred the responsibility for licensing from the magistrate to local councils, which are now termed the Licensing Authority. Included in the act was the potential for 24 hour opening, seven days a week. Further changes in April 2007 saw a ban on smoking in the work place in Wales, including the pub.

history of inn signs

Trade signs can be traced back to the Ancient Egyptians, with their use proliferating during Roman times. Normally Roman signs would be a relief carving in terracotta or stone, with a common symbol to indicate the trade, for example a dairy would be represented by a goat. With the Roman occupation of Britain the common Roman practice of hanging vine leaves outside a tavern to indicate it's purpose had to be replaced by the hanging of an evergreen bush – Britain's inclement weather did not favour the vine. If only ale was sold then the ale stake or the long pole used to stir the ale was displayed, if both wine and ale were on sale then both bush and pole

would be put out. With the abandonment of Britain by Rome the use of some form of signage persisted, with early tavern signs directed at the largely illiterate population based on religion, with the Cross, the Cross Keys, the Star and the Sun common images. By the 12th century it had become normal practice for inns to be individually named. However the symbol displayed soon became evidence of power, with the choice of image often being mandatory. In 1393 Richard II required his own personal emblem of the White Hart to be displayed to identify London inns to his official ale taster; in 1603, with James VI of Scotland becoming James I of England, all important buildings, including taverns, were required to display the Red Lion of Scotland. Development of inn signs mirrored the changes in society and trade as a whole, Railway taverns, Smugglers Haunts and Jolly Sailors being added to the signs of religion, nobility and royalty, and indication of place. The Three Horseshoes for example takes it's sign from that of the Worshipful Company of Farriers, usually thereby indicating the local landlord was also the blacksmith. In Wales the Red Dragon has became a favoured alternative to the Red Lion.

place-names

The study of place-names is a fascinating branch of local history in it's own right, indicating geographical features which may have vanished, patterns of former land ownership, forgotten buildings or former trades. However the current place name may be far removed from the original name, particularly where there is an anglicised form of an old Welsh name, for example Pembroke is derived from Pen Fro, the Welsh for Land's End. Welsh place-names are particularly expressive of geography, and can be highly poetic, for example Pwll Deri, pool of the oak trees. Some of the more common names are listed below:

Aber – river mouth, estuary
Afon – river
Ar – on, over
Bach/Fach – little
Ban/Fan(au) – peak, crest, beacon
Banc – bank
Barcud – kite
Bedd – grave
Bedw – birch
Blaen – top
Bre – hill
Bryn – hill
Bwlch – pass
Caer(au) – fort(s)
Canol – middle, centre
Cantref – hundred
(ancient land area)
Capel – chapel
Carn/Garn – cairn
Carreg, pl cerrig – rock, stone
Castell – castle
Cefn – ridge
Cil – nook, source of stream
Clawdd – ditch

Cleddau – sword
Clyn/Clun – meadow
Coch – red
Coed – wood
Coetref/Goetre – woodland, homestead
Cors/Gors – bog, marsh
Craig – rock, cliff
Crib – ridge
Croes – cross
Cromlech(au) – burial mound(s)
Cwm – valley
Cwrw – beer
Cyhoeddus – public
Dan – under
Darren – rocky hillside
Dau – two
Deri – oak tree
Dinas – hill fort
Dôl – meadow
Du/Ddu – black
Dŵr – water
Efail – smithy

Eglwys – church
Esgair – ridge
Ffordd – road
Ffrwd – stream, torrent
Ffynnon – fountain, well, spring
Gallt/Allt – hill, cliff, wood
Gelli – grove
Glan – river bank
Glas – blue, green
Gwaun – moor, meadow
Gwyn/Gwen – white
Gwynt – wind
Hafod – summer dwelling
Hen – old
Hendre – winter dwelling
Heol – road
Isaf – lower
Lan – ascent
Llaethdy – dairy
Llan, pl llanau – church, village
Llech – flat stone
Llyn – lake
Llwybr – path, track
Llwyd/lwyd – brown, grey; pale; hoary
Llwyn – grove, bush
Llydan – broad, wide
Maen – rock, stone
Maes – field
Marchog – horseman, rider, knight
Mawr/Fawr – great, big
Meddyg – doctor, physician
Melin – mill
Melyn – yellow
Moel/Foel – bare topped hill
Mwyn – ore, mineral

Mynydd – mountain
Nant – brook, stream
Newydd – new
Nos – night
Ogof – cave
Pant – hollow, valley
Porth – harbour
Picws – peak
Pwll – pool
Rhiw – hill
Rhos – moorland
Parc – field, park
Pen – head, top
Penlan – top of hill
Pentre – village
Plas – hall
Pont – bridge
Porth – harbour
Pwll – pool
Rhiw – hill
Rhos – moorland
Rhyd – ford
Sir – county, shire
Tafarn – inn
Tir – land, ground, territory
Traeth – beach
Tref – town, hamlet
Tri/tair – three
Tŷ – house
Uchaf – upper
Y/Yr – the
Yn – in
Ynys – island
Ysgol – school

A few notes on pronunciation:

c – k (hard)
ch – as in loch
dd – th as in that
f – v
ff – f
g – g (hard)
ll – pronounce l, keep tongue in position at roof of mouth, and hiss!
th – th as in think

There are 7 vowels, a, e, i, o, u, w and y. Pronunciation may be long or short.

w may be as in pool, or pull eg *cwm* (coom) – valley
y may be as in fun, or pin eg *y, yr* (u, ur) – the, *dyffryn* (dufrin) – valley

Many Welsh words change their pronunciation and spelling under certain circumstances, for example the initial consonant of many words may soften: b to f, c to g, m to f, p to b etc. Common examples of mutations are bach (little) to fach, mawr (big) to fawr, porth (harbour) to borth. Such mutations can make tracing words through a dictionary a little problematic.

One important Welsh word to know in a book on pub walks is *cwrw* (curoo) – beer.

touRist inpoRmation centRes

Cardigan – Theatr Mwldan	01239 613230
Goodwick – Ocean Lab, The Parrog	01348 872037
Fishguard – The Square	01437 776636
Haverfordwest – 19 Old Bridge	01437 763110
Milford Haven – 94 Charles Street	01646 690866
Newport – Banc Cottages, Long Street	01239 820912
Pembroke – Commons Road	01646 622388
St David's – Oriel Parc	01437 720392

Saundersfoot – The Barbecue, The Harbour   01834 813672
Tenby – Unit 2, Upper Park Road   01834 842402

the country code

Enjoy the countryside and respect it's life and work.
Guard against all risk of fire.
Fasten all gates.
Keep your dogs under close control.
Keep to public paths across farmland.
Use gates and stiles to cross fences, hedges and walls.
Leave livestock, crops and machinery alone.
Take your litter home.
Help to keep all water clean.
Protect wildlife, plants and trees.
Take special care on county roads.
Make no unnecessary noise.

hazards and problems
take notice, take care

The author and the publishers stresses that walkers should be aware of the dangers that may occur on all walks.
Check local weather forecast before walking; do not walk up into mist or low clouds.
Use local OS maps side by side with walking guides.
Wear walking boots and clothing.
Do not take any unnecessary risks – conditions can change suddenly and can vary from season to season.
Take special care when accompanied by children or dogs.
When walking on roads, ensure that you are conspicuous to traffic from either direction.
Please note that the terms 'easier', 'easy' are only used in this book in comparison to the most dangerous and challenging routes when you are out walking.

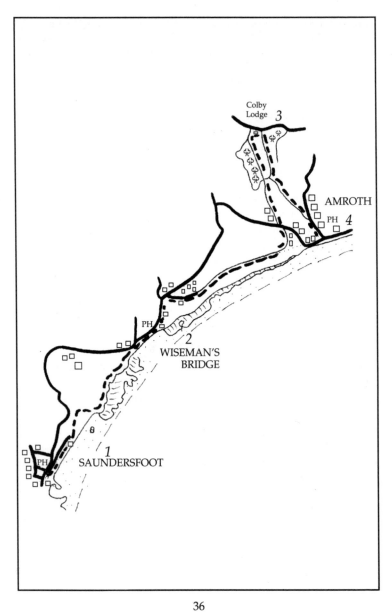

Colby
Lodge *3*

AMROTH

PH *4*

PH

2

WISEMAN'S
BRIDGE

PH

1

SAUNDERSFOOT

1. saundersfoot to wiseman's bridge and amroth

3.75 miles/6 kilometres

Note: At low tide it is possible to walk along the beach to Amroth; the beach route could be used to make a circular walk.

OS Maps: OS 1:25 000 South Pembrokeshire Outdoor Leisure 36.
Start: The Royal Oak in Saundersfoot.
Access: Saundersfoot can be easily reached from the A478 Kilgetty to Tenby road. Accessible by train and a number of bus routes – once at Amroth bus 351/350 will take you back to Saundersfoot.
Parking: Fee paying car park at Saundersfoot harbour.
Grade: Easy.

The Royal Oak Inn, Wogan Terrace, Saundersfoot
(01834 812546)
Long a popular pub the inn dates back to at least to the 19th century. A mid 19th century notice to lease the inn lists it having stables, gardens and brewhouse. The stables were still there in the early 1920s, when it was put up for auction. The benches outside give a fine view of the harbour and town, and are well favoured in summer months.

Wiseman's Bridge Inn (01834 813236)
Now a firm favourite with visitors, positioned as it is overlooking the beach, early 19th century patrons would no doubt have included many who worked the iron ore seams along the coast. The oldest part of the inn is to the left, adjacent to the road. There have been many alteration and extensions over the years, the most recent a cause of necessity after a fire started in the central heating boiler on Christmas Eve 2002 nearly destroyed the inn, the fire service managing to save the

oldest part. Accommodation available.

Amroth Arms, Amroth (01834 812480)
Purpose built circa 1870 the Amroth Arms took over the licence of the former Amroth Castle Arms, sited near to Amroth castle. The former inn was eventually demolished so Lord Kylsant could gain unimpeded access to Amroth castle for his car. Late 20th century alterations to the Amroth Arms combined the former two premises into one.

HISTORY NOTES
1. Saundersfoot
One of Pembrokeshire's most popular holiday destinations the harbour and sandy beach are fine attractions. Geologically the area forms part of the South Wales coalfield, and the belt of coal running across Pembrokeshire from Saundersfoot to Landshipping, Hook and Nolton has come to be termed the Daugleddau coalfield. Records show coal mining dating back to at least the 14th century, with coal forming the major county export by 1700. However there was no attempt to exploit the potential of the local anthracite – amongst the finest in the world, and much favoured by Queen Victoria for it's smokeless quality – until the 19th century. In 1829 the Saundersfoot Railway and Harbour Company was authorised, and by 1832 the harbour and one main line inland was in operation. Prior to the harbour's opening cargoes were loaded directly onto ships from the beach at Saundersfoot and Wiseman's Bridge. In 1842 the line was extended through three tunnels and along the cliff edge to Wiseman's Bridge, turning inland along Pleasant Valley to the Stepaside and Kilgetty collieries. Coal was hauled in drams by horse and oxen, until, in 1874, the line was re-laid and the locomotive *Rosalind* brought into service. The fortunes of the local collieries fluctuated, some closed, only to re-open, but by 1939 the coal industry here had ceased operations, and after 1945 the line was dismantled. Tourism is now the major

industry. The last Pembrokeshire colliery to close was at Hook, inland on the river Cleddau, in 1949. The old railway line along the coast from Saundersfoot is now part of the Coast Path. To Wiseman's Bridge is a short 1 mile / 1.75 kilometre walk, the tunnels cool and pleasant on warm summer days. Oh yes, the origins of the name Saundersfoot; not a lost foot, but a reference to a property in the name of a local family, foot being a topographical feature. Prior to industrialisation the town was no more than an handful of houses.

2. Wiseman's Bridge

Wiseman's Bridge takes it's name from one Andrew Wiseman who held half a knight's fee here, no Wiseman from the East this, but a Norman coloniser who reputedly accompanied an Earl of Pembroke, Aymer de Valence, from Normandy to Pembrokeshire in the early 14th century. There is a fine pebble banked storm beach, with at low tide the superb expanse of

Wiseman's Bridge

golden sand stretching some three miles / five kilometres from Amroth to Saundersfoot. A full scale mock landing for D Day took place here in 1943, with landing craft, barges, guns and soldiers scattered along the sea-lashed beach from Pendine to Saundersfoot. Eisenhower, Churchill and Montgomery were on site to supervise, Churchill being properly entertained by the Wiseman's Bridge Inn with sandwiches, Welsh cakes and tea. An earlier army found a similar use for the beach, when in 1153 the sands and cliffs echoed to the march of a Royal army of the sons of the Prince of West Wales, en route to surprise and destroy the Norman garrison at Tenby. The present Coast Path along the cliff top was once the main county road from Saundersfoot to Amroth, but the collapse of iron ore workings in the cliffs below made the road impracticable.

3. Colby Lodge

Colby Lodge was built for the industrialist John Colby in 1803 to a Nash design. The woodland gardens were laid out by Samuel Kay, who bought the estate in the late 19th century. A good number of the original rhododendrons planted then, many brought back from the Himalayas by Kay's brother, have survived the years to grace the woodland slopes. The natural woodland here is believed to be a remnant of the great medieval forest of Coedrath which extended from Saundersfoot to Amroth. The timber would have been a useful source of fuel, the poor only using coal when they could not afford wood. However with timber running short by the 1600s use would have been made of the local anthracite, and both anthracite and iron ore were extensively mined on the estate by John Colby during the early and mid 19th century. Some of the old workings can still be traced in the grounds, though little remains of the area's natural resources. Transport of coal from inland collieries to Saundersfoot harbour during their heyday in the 19th and early 20th centuries was, away from the railway lines, by carts, many pulled by teams of oxen and horses. As a result many roads were deeply rutted and often impassable.

Turnpike Trusts were set up to improve conditions, but toll prices on the roads were so high that the local populace was alienated. Toll gates were smashed by rioters, that at nearby Killanow crossroads being no exception. The Killanow notice board, giving prices for animals, carts and men, has survived and has found it's way to Colby Lodge's café. The eight acre garden, though not the Lodge itself, is now in the hands of the National Trust, and is open from March/April through to October – lots of estate paths and vistas to enjoy. The garden has two champion trees – a Japanese Red Cedar and a False Cypress both being the tallest trees for their species registered in Britain and Ireland.

4. Amroth

The name Amroth *(Am-rath)* may mean on, or near, the river Rath, believed to have been the name of one of the parish's boundary streams, or on, or near the fort, and in various spellings can be traced back to at least 1220. Amroth's history as a village, however, dates back only as far as the mid 19th century. Prior to this a traveller journeying along the coast would have found only a scattering of houses near the church, or the gentry mansions. However Amroth was on the edge of the Daugleddau coalfield, and with 19th century industrial expansion both coal and iron ore were in demand. Between Amroth and Saundersfoot there were some fifty patches, each worked by two men who dug for iron ore in the cliffs. To the north of the village there developed the coal mining collieries of Coombes and Castlepark, small brothers of the larger Bonville's Court Colliery near Saundersfoot, and the Stepaside collieries. Amroth developed into a miners' village, close by the cliffs that gave many work.

The sea has always been jealous of the land here. Some 7,000 years ago there was a forest stretching far out from the present shoreline, the petrified remains still visible at exceptionally low tides. More recently, in the 1930s, the village at it's western end had houses on both sides of the road, but the storms soon put paid to their bright optimism, and they had to be demolished as unsafe. The present system of groynes along the beach are a modern attempt to further deny the sea. On clear days good views of Caldey island, Tenby and Saundersfoot on the right, with the Gower peninsula and the Worm's Head framing Carmarthen Bay to the left. Amroth castle, marked on the OS map, is recent, dating from the early 19th century, though it is on, or near the site of the Norman Eareweare castle, all traces of which have now vanished. The Norman castle was dealt a fatal blow by Prince Llywelyn, who in the early 1200s was in the process of reclaiming, albeit temporarily, much of South West Wales from Norman colonisers. Rebuilt at various times, and in various forms, the present castle has been converted to holiday flats, with caravans and chalets in the grounds. One early 19th century resident and local worthy rejoiced in the delightful title of the Reverend Thomas Shrapnel Biddulph. One wonders if his sermons were as explosive as his name suggests.

WALK DIRECTIONS [-] indicates history note

1. Starting from the Royal Oak (looking inland from the harbour car park the Royal Oak is to the right, on the corner of Wogan Terrace and High Street) walk down hill towards the harbour, tuning left before the beach to gain the Strand. Continue along the Strand (route of the old railway line) to leave Saundersfoot [1] through a series of tunnels to reach Coppet Hall and Wiseman's Bridge [2].

2. Walk past the Wiseman's Bridge Inn and continue uphill on the road, taking the first turning right. Shortly again turn right onto a No Through Road, to shortly gain a well defined track. Continue, passing a caravan park on the left. After just over 0.5 miles/0.75 kilometres the Coast Path continues right over a stile. Continue instead ahead on the Public Path to reach the Amroth road.

3. Turn left, cross the road, and shortly turn right onto a Public Path, passing in front of houses. Continue past the houses to

reach a grassy path. Good views of Colby Lodge ahead, in the trees. Continue ahead and downhill to meet a T junction of paths. Continue directly ahead to reach Colby Lodge [3] on your right.

4. Once at the lodge, either by walking right along the minor road or through the grounds, gain the other side of the building. Follow the path leading back the way you have come, but this time with the lodge to your right, to reach a minor road. Bear right to continue through Amroth [4] to reach the sea front by a bus stop, and by the Amroth Arms.

FACILITIES

All available in Saundersfoot and Amroth, including lots more pubs!

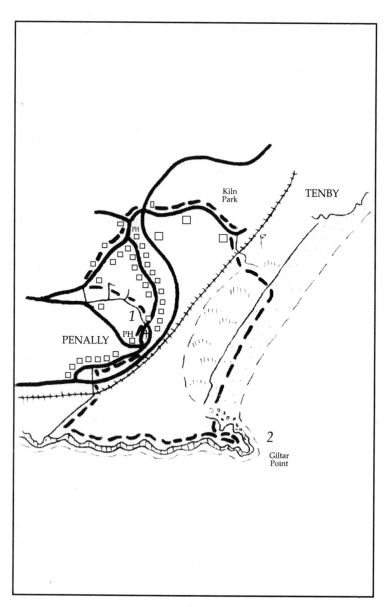

Kiln
Park

TENBY

PH

1

PENALLY

PH

2

Giltar
Point

2. penally

4.5 miles/7.25 kilometres

Note: Part of this walk goes through Penally firing range (by Giltar Point) – check the range is open before walking. Red flags fly when in use!

OS Maps: OS 1:25 000 South Pembrokeshire Outdoor Leisure 36.
Start: Cross Inn, Penally.
Access: Penally is situated on the A4139, just south west of Tenby. Buses 358 from Tenby to Pembroke Dock and 349 Tenby to Haverfordwest stop at Penally, as does the train from Swansea and Tenby to Pembroke Dock.
Parking: There is no parking at the Cross Inn, however there is possible parking by the church, close by.
Grade: Moderate.

Cross Inn (01834 844665)
Formerly two cottages the Cross Inn opened for business in 1867. It has an attractive interior, with outside seating giving fine views of the coast.

Paddock Inn (01834 843783)
A comparative newcomer from the 1970s the Paddock Inn was formerly Holloway farm, the farmhouse itself dating from the 17th century. Patio garden to front, with, inside, an attractive and welcoming stone fireplace. Normally open evenings only.

HISTORY NOTES

1. Penally

Penally is clustered around it's hill, a fitting backdrop to the glorious sweep of Tenby's south beach. The present name is a corruption of Penalun, head of the river Alun, now culverted. St Teilo, an influential 6th century contemporary of St David, was reputedly born here. There was a monastery in the area at one time, but the site is now lost. The ruins in the grounds of Penally Abbey hotel may be those of a chapel dedicated to St Deiniol, with whom the well, strikingly set in the lane wall opposite, is associated. The well may be a survival of a pre-Christian past, for wells, rivers and sacred trees were objects of devotion in Celtic religion. They would have had their own particular god, and their cult would be maintained by local druids, who would arrange for any particular public or private sacrifice. The Norman church, in it's splendid setting amongst the palms, is 13th century, with a 14th century porch and probable 16th century tower. It is dedicated to St Nicholas of Myra, patron saint of seafarers. There is, in the south transept, a fine and rare sandstone tomb, with, on either side of a worn Calvary cross, the heads of a man and woman. The inscription, in Norman French, is to William and Isamay de Naunton.

There are three 9th and 10th century crosses in the church which would originally have stood outside in the present churchyard. They may have been carved for the monastery. The broken shafts of two are now all that remain, the third is complete and has a fine, delicate wheel headed cross. The complete stone has Celtic knotwork culminating, in the front, in a vine scroll, whilst a second shows what appear to be reptiles devouring each other. These Celtic crosses provide evidence for the early history of Christianity, set up to commemorate individuals many have survived, whereas the early religious cells have long since vanished or been built over. Penally's crosses are lighter in touch, and more finely lyrical in spirit than the two other major Pembrokeshire Celtic crosses at Carew and

Nevern, which are heavier and more powerful in feeling. Penally is now a flourishing and modern village, after all the first house in Pembrokeshire to install electricity was here! It has grown much in size and popularity over the last half a century or so.

Penally has had a rich history of human occupation. Hoyle's Mouth, on the north side of Penally at Longbury Bank, is a natural limestone cave cut out by the action of water. Like other limestone caves here, at Cat's Hole near Monkton Pembroke, and on Caldey island (then a hill on the Carmarthen plain), they provided shelter for families and clans of Stone Age peoples moving north from Europe. Arriving some 30,000 years ago, before the onset of the last great ice sheet, they may have been forced to retreat before the shifting ice, to return again from 12,500 years ago. Living at, or near, the cave entrance, these hunter gatherers shared territory with cave lions, cave bears, hyenas, and woolly rhinoceros. Looking out from their fire warm caves they would have seen land that stretched out across the great plain of the Bristol Channel to beyond present day Ireland. Across the great plain, tundra or temperate dependent on the shifting ice, roamed mammoth, elk and auroch, which provided a great source of food and clothes. Finds here at Hoyle's Mouth, and at other caves close by, include reindeer and horse, cave bear, woolly mammoth and hyena, as well as simple tools.

By 10,000 years ago the last of the ice from the Irish Sea glacier had melted, and Milford Haven's river valley was a flood. With the drowning of the coastal areas Pembrokeshire began to assume it's present shape. The river Ritec, between Penally and Tenby, was at one time a tidal river, and during the Middle Ages ships and barges made their way three miles / five kilometres up river to St Florence. From 1811 to 1820 an embankment was built across it's mouth to create new pasture land. The 1863 Pembroke to Tenby railway was laid across the top of this embankment. The result is extensive reedbeds and

Penally and Tenby

marshland. Tenby marsh and the surrounding area are home to the Tenby daffodil; unique to the area it has a fine golden yellow sheen and a trumpet longer than the surrounding petals.

Tenby itself, with it's 13th century castle and town walls, has to be one of the most favoured spots in Wales. An important fishing and trading centre in Tudor and Stuart times Tenby's later fortunes, and elegance, as a holiday resort owe much to the efforts of Sir William Paxton in the early 19th century. Tenby's south beach was the favoured landing place of the peregrini, early saints and pilgrims who would have landed here, en route to St David's, Whitesands Bay and Ireland. The beach is backed by the Burrows, a dune system as fine as Freshwater West's on Pembrokeshire's western facing coast, and the oldest golf course in Wales.

2. Giltar Point and Caldey Island
Giltar Point forms part of Pembrokeshire's magnificent southern limestone coast. Characterised by short springy turf

this coastal section makes for easy walking. Caldey island, from *kald-ey* (spring water), as the Norse called it, was also known as Ynys Byr, the island of Pyr, the abbot of the first religious house in the early 6th century. Most of the present abbey and church were built by the Benedictines from 1910 to 1912. The island was sold off on 1926, and is now home to the Cistercians, former holders of Tintern and Fountains Abbeys. One notable visitor to the island was the Emperor Haile Selassie of Ethiopia, who found a brief refuge here during the Second World War. St Margaret's island, close by, has a nationally important cormorant colony, alongside numbers of razorbills and guillemots. The ruined buildings are old quarrymen's cottages, converted in Victorian times from a former medieval chapel. The island was last quarried in the early 1850s. Given clear weather good views south of Lundy island and the coast of Devon.

WALK DIRECTIONS [-] indicates history note

1. Starting from the Cross Inn in Penally [1] walk up the lane the short distance to Penally Abbey Hotel, keeping the church on the right. Bear left at the hotel – sign here marked *Penally Nature Trail*. After a short distance St Deiniol's well is passed on the left.

2. At the entrance to Penally Manor leave the lane through an iron gate on the right (or cross the stile), and ascend on a woodland path to enter a field. Great views of Tenby and Carmarthen Bay now open up.

3. Bear diagonally right on a visible path across the field, and at the field boundary bear slightly left and downhill to a metal gate. Go through the gate and descend on a grassy and steep track to reach the tarmac road by Frankleston House.

4. Turn right and follow the road to the T junction opposite the Paddock Inn. Turn left and continue bearing right to the main A4139. Cross and leaving the main road continue ahead going between the garage and a private house to reach the main route through Kiln Park. Walking man and cycle route signposts here.

5. Continue on the main route through the caravan park, passing the remains of impressive kilns on your right. At the small roundabout bear right to pass in front of the shop. After a short distance bear right – there are signposts here indicating cycle route and *To the Beach*, and a sign *Guillemot* indicating this particular part of the park.

6. Continue over a railway bridge and continue ahead on the track through the golf course to reach Tenby's south beach. Bear right and cross the beach to reach steps leading up to the path leading to Giltar Point [2].

7. Once at Giltar Point bear right and continue along the coastal path through Ministry of Defence land until a guard post is reached. Bear right here, and continue downhill, keeping the fence on your left.

8. Continue under a railway bridge to reach the main road. Cross and continue across a field to reach the minor road through Penally. Bear right to reach the starting point.

FACILITIES
All facilities available in Penally.

3. MANORBIER

6 miles/9.5 kilometres

OS Maps: OS 1:25 000 South Pembrokeshire Outdoor Leisure 36.
Start: Castle Inn in Manorbier.
Access: Manorbier is reached from the A4139 Pembroke to Tenby road, and is equidistant between the 2 towns. Buses 333/358 Tenby – Pembroke and 349 Tenby – Pembroke – Haverfordwest stop at Manorbier. Manorbier train station (service Swansea – Tenby – Pembroke Dock) is just over a mile/1.5 kilometres north of the village.
Parking: Either free parking in front of *The Dak* at Manorbier bay (see map), or in the National Park car park below Manorbier Castle – seasonal charge. Parking also possible in Manorbier.
Grade: Moderate. Coastal path, field, green lane and road – there is a fairly steep section at East Moor Cliff.

Castle Inn (01834 871268)
Since the late 18th century there have been a number of pubs opened and closed in the village; the Castle Inn being the survivor. Two pubs, no doubt hoping that tourism would help boost sales, opened in the late twentieth century, but they lasted for only a few years. Up until 1931 the house next door to the present inn was the Lion, the favoured haunt of local farmers, whilst villagers preferred the Castle. Now all sup at the Castle. Garden to the back of the pub.

HISTORY NOTES
1. Manorbier
The origin of Manorbier as a place name is uncertain. One interpretation has it as the Maenor Bŷr, that is a holding of land by Pyrrus or Pŷr, the 6th century first Abbot of Caldey island monastery. It is known that Caldey had farming estates on the mainland. Not much is known of Pyrrus, though it is known that after a night of too much local wine he drowned in the

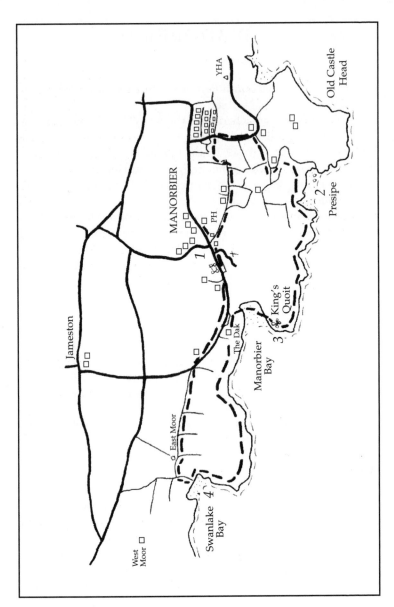

Old Castle Head

YHA

MANORBIER

PH

Presipe

2

1

King's Quoit

3

The Dak

Manorbier Bay

Jameston

East Moor

4

Swanlake Bay

West Moor

Manorbier Castle

Abbey fishpond! The present spelling dates from the 1860s. The Norman history of Manorbier began when Odo de Barri was given lands here as a reward for military service, sometime shortly after the Norman invasion of Pembrokeshire in 1093. His son William began the building of the stone castle in the 12th century, though most of it's construction dates from between 1230 to 1260. More of a fortified mansion than a fortress new farming techniques were introduced which added new types of food, with a surplus for sale, to the oats, barley, meat and dairy produce normally consumed.

To the Norman colony were brought Flemish builders, farmers and tradesmen to supplant the local Welsh. An open field system was introduced, with a water mill for grinding corn, a fishpond, orchard, deer park and dovecote added. The dovecote still stands, reached on the footpath/road below the castle (located nearly opposite the National Park car park entrance). It is just past the ruins of a second, later mill. The original mill and fishpond were situated in the valley between the castle and the church. Manorbier castle was fortunate never to be attacked, partly due to the Welsh connections of the de Barris, partly because it was out of the way of the more imposing fortress castles. Nearly a ruin by the 19th century it was rescued in the 1880s by the talented renovations of J R Cobb.

The church across the valley is originally Norman, it's imposing tower (now painted white) dating from 1270. Dedicated to St James the Great it was restored between 1867 and 1870. Worth a visit for it's unusual interior. Like many early ecclesiastical buildings it has a circular graveyard. Like it's near neighbours Tenby and Saundersfoot it's popularity as a seaside resort began from the mid 18th century and the building of the Pembroke to Tenby railway in 1863. Manorbier came to be seen as a little more exclusive than Tenby. In the centre of the village, opposite the Post Office, is the restored Bier House, nothing to do with the history of the village or the origin of it's name (or the local pub), but built in 1900 to house the parish bier! Key available to view if locked – see notice.

OF GERALD OF WALES AND WELSH HOSPITALITY

Manorbier's most famous son was born Gerald de Barri, son of William de Barri and Angharad de Carew, granddaughter of the last Prince of South Wales, Rhys ap Tewdwr, circa 1146. Scholar, intellectual, politician and ecclesiastic, he was made Archdeacon of Brecon at 28, lectured in law at the University of Paris, and was chaplain and tutor to the young Richard I and King John.

He spent much of his life campaigning to become Bishop of St David's and struggling with Henry II to create a Welsh National Church. His failure to do so was probably due him being too Welsh and too capable for Henry's uses. If this was not enough he still found time to pen 17 books, of which the *Description of Wales* and *Journey through Wales*, and the *History and Topography of Ireland*, are the best known, and which are still in print. His life earned him the title of Gerald of Wales, or Giraldus Cambrensis. He died in 1223, at the fine age of 77.

In his books he writes lively and entertaining prose, extolling the virtues of the Welsh, and his homeland of Wales and Manorbier. Here he is, in his *Description of Wales* from circa 1191, on the virtues of the Welsh, in this case their hospitality and generosity. *When you travel there is no question of your asking for accommodation or of their offering it: you just march into a house and hand over your weapons to the person in charge. They give you water so that you may wash your feet and that means you are a guest ... Guests who arrive early in the day are entertained until nightfall by girls who play to them on the harp ...*

Times are no longer what they were.

2. Presipe

Presipe has a fine, sandy beach, with no access to it by car. The many stacks and rocks make it an interesting area for rock pool exploration, with plenty of sea anemones, crabs, starfish and those chameleons of the rock pool fish world, the blenny. The Atlantic gales and tides which hammer this southern coast can leave the occasional visitor. I have seen jelly fish stranded by the tide, decked out in fine white, purple and yellow, with thin, neat black lines for a border, and tentacles splayed out to the side like silver chains. Old Castle Head, above, was once an Iron Age fort. During World War 1 airships, acting in accord with the hydrophone station on Carn Llidi on St David's Head, used to leave for photographic reconnaissance, on constant lookout for submarines. The site is now a Royal Artillery Range. Good views south to Lundy island on a clear day.

3. King's Quoit
King's Quoit is a Neolithic cromlech, or burial chamber, dating from circa 3,000 BC. Unusual, in that the main distribution of the cromlechs are on the northern coast, use may well have been made of a loose ledge from the ridge above to act as a capstone. However one of the three supporting pillars has fallen. There is no record of any skeleton being found. There have been both Mesolithic and Neolithic flint finds at Manorbier and around the headland at Swanlake Bay – the tides then would have been further out, away from the present shoreline, and at exceptionally low tides there are the remains of a prehistoric forest.

4. Swanlake Bay
Swanlake Bay, like Presipe, is another isolated beach, accessible only from the Coast Path, or on footpaths from East and West Moor farms. It's sandy beach and isolation make it a popular alternative to the more crowded beaches of Freshwater East or Manorbier. Both East Moor and West Moor farms were original Norman land grant farms, under the lordship of Manorbier.

WALK DIRECTIONS [-] indicates history note
1. From the Castle Inn in Manorbier [1] walk down the hill towards Manorbier Bay, turning left by the Castlemead Hotel.

2. Follow the road past the houses onto a farm lane. Ignore the turning right and continue left to reach a stile giving access to a green lane – there is a well preserved limekiln on the left just past the stile.

3. Continue straight ahead on the green lane to cross stiles and meet a short path bearing left uphill into a field. Follow the path and cross the field to a road – there is a children's play area on the left en route.

4. Turn right on to the road and continue uphill to turn right across a stile just before the boundary of Manorbier Royal Artillery Range – the road itself continues around left to Skrinkle Haven and a youth hostel. You are now on the Coast Path.

5. Follow the boundary fence, to cross two fields, and then turn left over a stile into a third field. Go straight ahead, bearing slightly left, to reach the stile giving access to the cliff path.

8. Continue on the Coast Path, passing Presipe on your left [2] – steep steps will lead you down to the beach – and follow the Path for a mile/1.5 kilometres around to King's Quoit [3] and Manorbier Bay.

9. Cross Manorbier beach to cross a stream by a stone footbridge and climb the steps cut into the rock to gain the path passing in front of a parking bay. Follow the path through *The Dak* grounds and continue on the Coast Path for well over a mile/1.5 kilometres to Swanlake Bay [4].

10. Go through the metal gate at the head of the beach and immediately bear diagonally right uphill away from the beach, to shortly bear sharp right, ignoring the section that continues ahead, and continue uphill to a field.

11. Keep to the right field edge to shortly cross right a stone stile, or go though a metal kissing gate, into another field. Keep to the left field edge to meet another gate giving access to the farm lane at East Moor. Turn right, then shortly left to meet another stone stile/metal gate.

12. Continue ahead across fields, keeping to the left edge, to meet the minor road leading to Manorbier. Turn right on to the road and follow it down to Manorbier and uphill to the starting point.

FACILITIES
Manorbier offers a Post Office and shop, BT telephone, and cafe. Public toilets by the castle entrance, and at the National Park car park. Manorbier castle and garden open daily Easter to end September. Picnic site and youth hostel at Skrinkle Haven.

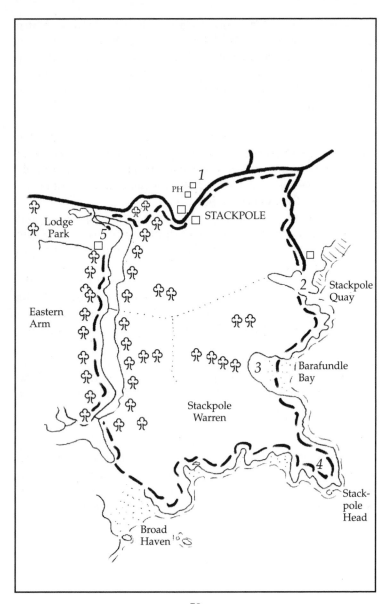

PH

1

STACKPOLE

Lodge
Park

5

Eastern
Arm

2 Stackpole
Quay

Barafundle
Bay

3

Stackpole
Warren

4

Stack-
pole
Head

Broad
Haven

4. Stackpole

6 miles/9.5 kilometres

Note: Can be combined with the Bosherston walk to make for a longer circuit.

OS Maps: OS 1:25 000 South Pembrokeshire Outdoor Leisure 36.
Start: Stackpole village.
Access: Stackpole can be reached on the minor road between Freshwater East and the B4319 Pembroke to Castlemartin road. Bus routes 364 and 387/388 Pembroke Dock – Stackpole – Angle.
Parking: There is a car park to the rear of the Stackpole Inn, and also a small parking area in the village opposite the pub.
Grade: Moderate.

Stackpole Inn (01646 672324)
This attractive inn is made up of two 17th century cottages which formerly comprised the local Post Office. To the left of the main entrance, set in the wall, is the old King George V letter box. Use of local materials has contributed much to the character of the pub – the bar is of local Welsh slate, the beams made of ash from the National Trust's Stackpole estate. Fine attractive garden. Prior to the selling off of the Cawdor estate there was no pub in Stackpole – the Cawdors had no liking for alcohol, and it was not until late last century that a local builder created the Armstrong Arms, named after himself. 2002 saw the name change to it's present one. En suite accommodation available.

HISTORY NOTES
1. Stackpole village
Stackpole takes it's name from the Norse *stac*, meaning a rock, and *pollr*, a small inlet. The rocks in question are Star and Church Rocks in Broad Haven. Testimony to the power of the

59

Stackpole Inn

local landowners, the Cawdors, the village once stood on the opposite side of the lake from now demolished Stackpole Court, but because it spoilt the view from the mansion the village was moved to it's present location some two hundred years ago.

2. Stackpole Quay

The quay was built inside a limestone quarry by Lord Cawdor in the late 1700s to help export quarried limestone by local sailing ships, enormous quantities of coal for nearby Stackpole Court being landed in return. No longer commercially used it still provides a base for local boat owners and canoeists. The quarry itself now forms the National Trust's car park.

3. Barafundle Bay

As attractive as it's name suggests Barafundle Bay is one of Pembrokeshire's finest beaches, if not it's finest. The fact that it can only be reached on foot seems to add to it's popularity. The wall and steps down from Stackpole Quay were built by the Cawdors, giving access to what was at one time their own private beach.

4. Stackpole Head and Warren

One of the finest stretches of limestone coast in southern Pembrokeshire clear days give fine views across to Caldey island and the Gower peninsula. Just beyond Stackpole Quay the grays of the Carboniferous Limestone give way to the red rocks of Old Red Sandstone which stretch around the coast to Manorbier and beyond. Manorbier's castle can be picked out, it's grey walls contrasting with the striated red rocks and yellow sands, and on fine days, the deep blue of the sea. Good views also of the natural arches which stand out from the rocks between the headland and Barafundle Bay. The walk on to Broad Haven is exhilarating, the sheer limestone cliffs contrasting with the caves, stacks and wave cut platforms cut out by the sea, and the blow holes formed by the collapse of the limestone. The cliffs are good rock climbing quality, and climbers' pitches can be picked out all along the coast. The short springy turf is favoured by that rare member of the crow family, with it's red beak and legs, the chough, while the cliffs and stacks offer nesting sites to gulls and fulmars, kittiwakes, razorbills and guillemots. Stackpole Warren, as the name suggests, has always been much favoured by the local rabbits, and until the 1950s natural and artificial warrens were used by rabbit catchers. The short turf here, and the many wild flowers, owes it's evolution to the rabbit. The dune system is stable, with sand continuing to be blown up from Broad Haven.

5. Stackpole Court and Bosherston lakes

Or rather the site of it, for the mansion was demolished in 1963. Prior to the building of Stackpole Court it had been the site of an 11th century castle, built by a Norman lord, Elidur de Stackpole. Ownership of the castle and land passed through the centuries to the Vernon and Lort families, until it passed to the Cawdors in the late 17th century by means of a fine romance. Gilbert Lort, heir to the estate, was at Cambridge with Alexander Campbell, the heir to Cawdor in Scotland, their castle being at Nairn, near Inverness (one previous thane of Cawdor was, a Shakespeare notes, Macbeth). It was the custom for the two of them to travel to Stackpole together, Campbell then travelling on by ship to Fort William, and on across the Great Glen to Cawdor. On one occasion storms delayed Campbell, who then had time to meet and fall in love with Elizabeth, Gilbert Lort's sister. They were married in 1689. When Elizabeth inherited Stackpole from her brother the estate passed to the Campbells. It was their great grandson who was created Baron Cawdor in 1796, his son becoming the first Earl Cawdor.

It was John Campbell, the son of Gilbert and Elizabeth, who demolished the existing castellated building, creating a more fitting Georgian mansion on the site in 1735 (it was extended and partly rebuilt in 1843). It was he who moved Stackpole village to it's present site. The stable block too was given attention, and built in a "princely" style (though it too was rebuilt in 1843-4). Bosherston lakes, or the lily ponds as they are better known, were created between roughly 1760 and 1840 as a landscape feature. As with all followers of the landscape movement no estate was complete without woods and park, nor without ornamental features. Lodge Park, opposite the entrance to the court, was continuously re-designed, with the addition of plantings of exotic trees; opposite the court, on the other side of the lake, a new deer park was created in the late 18th century. Lodge Park Wood still has it's curved stone rustic seat, and summer house, whilst grotto and ruined stone arch adorn Caroline Grove. The old ice house in Lodge Park Wood has been restored – ice being used in pantries and larders to preserve food. The ice itself, and hard packed snow, was stored between layers of straw.

By the 1960s Stackpole Court had become difficult to maintain, with no grants available for repair, and penal taxation, and it was accordingly demolished. In July 1976, as part of a Treasury agreement on death duties, the property was transferred to the nation, the National Trust acquiring some 1992.5 acres of the estate, including the nearby coastline and

Freshwater West, under the Neptune Campaign. In 1992-3 the National Trust, in partnership with South Pembrokeshire District Council, converted the old stable block, which had survived the demolition, into flats – they are the attractive buildings to the side of the former court, surmounted by the clock tower. The Brewery and Game Larder also survived the demolition; the Game Larder, in front of the stable block, has an exhibition of the estate's history, together with photos.

WALK DIRECTIONS [-] indicates history note

1. Starting from Stackpole village [1] continue uphill on the Freshwater East road, taking the first turning right and walk down to reach Stackpole Quay [2] 1 mile/1.5 kilometres away. Attractive limekiln on the right just before Stackpole Quay.

2. Leave the road at a short stone wall where the road continues right to the National Trust car park and join the Coast Path leading down steps to the quay itself. Cross in front of the National Trust tearooms (the old coal house) and continue up steps and follow the path onto Barafundle Bay [3].

3. Once at Barafundle cross the beach and ascend steps to the path leading to Stackpole Head [4]. There is a path which gives a short cut across the headland, and which avoids the longer route around the coast – however this would be to miss some fine scenery!

4. Whichever route you choose continue to Broad Haven, and either walk along the beach or the Coast Path to head inland away from the sea. Continue to the lily ponds, and keeping the first lake on your left follow the path to reach Grassy Bridge. Cross and turning right follow the path on the left of the lake – known as the Eastern Arm.

5. Follow the path alongside the Eastern and Upper Eastern Arms to reach the site of Stackpole Court [5]. The path is edged in early Spring with the whites of wild garlic, adding their own distinctive aroma to the spring air. There is a hide on the right just before Stackpole Court.

6. Head for the road leading away from the buildings; however just before the turning bay bear right downhill on a path and crossing by a bridge meet a T junction. Bear right into Caroline Grove, and just before the grotto and ruined arch again bear right to cross a boardwalk. Continue past a hide, and shortly bear left.

7. Continue through the woodland to reach a minor road. Bear right and continue the short distance uphill to the starting point.

FACILITIES

National Trust tearooms and toilets at Stackpole Quay. The Trust have holiday cottages at Stackpole Quay.

5. Bosherston

4 miles/6.5 kilometres

Note: Part of this walk is within Castlemartin Range. Check in Bosherston, or with Tourist Offices, Information Centres, or under Public Notices in the Western Telegraph, to see if firing is scheduled. Red flags fly when in use.

OS Maps: OS 1:25 000 South Pembrokeshire Outdoor Leisure 36.
Start: St Govan's Country Inn in Bosherston.
Access: Bosherston is reached on the minor road from the B4319 Pembroke to Castlemartin road. Bus routes 364 and 387/388 Pembroke Dock – Bosherston – Angle.
Parking: Limited parking at St Govan's Inn – there is a larger car park to the right of Bosherston church. Parking also possible at Broad Haven (seasonal charge), and at St Govan's Chapel.
Grade: Easy – footpath, beach, field and grassland. Some road walking.

St Govan's Country Inn (01646 661643)

Like it's neighbouring village of Stackpole Bosherston once formed part of the Stackpole estate, and was subject to the estate owners, the Cawdors, dislike of alcohol. It was not until the estate was sold that a pub could open here, St Govan's Country Inn opening, after much local debate, in 1977 – the building itself dates from this time. A popular haunt for the local climbers, as the photographs on the wall testify, as well as for locals and visitors. Freshly caught mackerel and bass in season, home made cawl. Good vegetarian choice. En suite accommodation available. Pembrokeshire CAMRA Real Ale award winner.

HISTORY NOTES
1. Bosherston

A pretty place to while away a summer's afternoon, with the

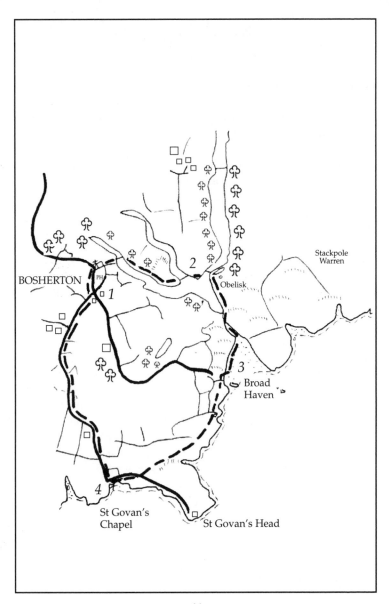

Stackpole
Warren

Obelisk

BOSHERTON

1

2

3

Broad
Haven

4

St Govan's
Chapel

St Govan's Head

Olde Worlde Café and lily ponds nearby. Bosherston, Bosher's Town, was given to Bosher, in the retinue of de Stackpole who came over with William the Conqueror. In the 13th century it was known as Stackpole Bosher, to distinguish it from nearby Stackpole Elidyr. The church of St Michael and All Angels is late 13th century, built on the site of an earlier church. It was restored in 1855 by the Cawdor family. The font is Norman. There is a preaching, or Calvary cross, in the grounds, set into a two tier stone base. It's probable date is 14th century. The head at the intersection is that of Christ, and may suggest that it was originally a crucifix that had been mutilated during the Reformation, and, minus it's original stem, been converted to a Calvary cross. The church gateway has what are known as *Cock and Hen* gateposts, formerly common in the county at the entrances to farms and churches. The two gateposts are topped by stones of different sizes, the largest being the hen. The idea is believed to be Viking in origin – they had the friendly habit of displaying the heads of their enemies, male and female, on their stockades.

2. Bosherston lily ponds

The lily ponds are an exhilarating area, particularly in May and June when they are at their best. A series of inter-connecting fish ponds comprising the western, middle and eastern arms they extend over some eighty acres and were created between the late 18th and early 19th centuries by the Earl Cawdor to enhance the Stackpole estate. The drowned river valley is protected from the sea by a shingle bank and sand bar, and as further guard against natural accidents, a man made retaining wall. The resultant freshwater pools provide good entertainment for coarse fishing; pike predominate, but there are plenty of perch, tench, eels and roach to try the temper. Three delightful footbridges give access. Well frequented by herons, swans, coots, mallards, moorhens and the occasional kingfisher. Lady Margaret's Seat, giving a grand view over the area, is a late 19th century obelisk with four stone seats built into it. There is a fine

Lily ponds

3rd to 4th century BC Iron Age fort, known as Fishponds Camp, situated between the western and middle arms of the lily ponds. At that time the valley would have been open to the sea, and would have provided a good protected landing place for new settlers. The site is now overgrown with bramble and gorse and cannot be reached.

3. Broad Haven

Broad Haven is frequently called Broad Haven South to distinguish it from Broad Haven on St Brides Bay. It is a fine sandy beach, backed by sand dunes, the youngest dunes those closest to the sea. The dune area of Stackpole Warren, as it's name implies, has been home to generations of rabbits, and it's warrens, both natural and artificial, were well used by rabbit catchers up until the 1950s. The Warren is still fed by sand blown up from Broad Haven – all dunes require dry sand, with sufficient wind to drive it ashore. Once these conditions are right then marram grass can send out it's roots, and the accumulations of sand colonised and stabilised. Dunes offer the opportunity to view the progression from bare ground through to stable dunes, and on to thin turf and thicket. Plenty of plant life for exploration, the blues of viper's bugloss giving way to the red berries of sea buckthorn. The smaller of the two rocks guarding Broad Haven is Church Rock. It's profile, viewed from the car park area, bears an uncanny resemblance to King Kong. Good views from the sea's edge of the sheer cliffs of Stackpole Head and the softer outlines of Caldey island.

4. St Govan's Chapel and Castlemartin peninsula

St Govan's chapel, built into the limestone cliffs at the only accessible point along this stretch of coast, has to be one of the best hermit's chapels in Britain. Despite legends connecting him with Sir Gawaine of Arthurian fame, St Govan is believed to be Gobhan or Gobban, the 6th century Abbot of Dairinis monastery in Wexford, Ireland. It is not known why he came to Pembrokeshire – perhaps there was a connection with St Ailbe, founder of Dairinis monastery, who originated from Solva, near St David's – whatever the reason he stayed the rest of his life in his cell in meditation and preaching. He died in 586. The present chapel dates from rebuilding in the 13th century (with a little recent help from the National Park), though the walls and altar may date from the 6th century. Of interest is the doorway to the north of the altar, which gives access to a small chamber cut into the rock. Outside the chapel there is a rock boulder known as Bell Rock. Legend tells that St Govan was given a silver bell which was stolen by pirates. St Govan duly prayed for it's return, and accordingly it was retrieved by angels and placed inside the boulder for safekeeping. The rock, on being struck by St Govan, gave out a note a thousand times louder than that of the original bell. To the south of the chapel there is a well, now dry, but which was visited until the 1850s for wishes and healing.

The Coastguard lookout on St Govan's Head is only used in rough weather. The limestone cliffs from Linney Head to

Stackpole Head are amongst the finest in Britain, and provide fine climbing opportunities. Cliff caves, still extant, were well favoured by late Mesolithic, Neolithic and Bronze Age peoples, who have left behind bones of red deer, wolf, pig and fox, as well as pottery, flint and the odd human bone as evidence of their presence. They may well have been good rock climbers, however access to the higher caves was easier then because the lower sea levels and the freezing and thawing of the rock face had resulted in cliff shattering, and the formation of rubble slopes, often reaching from the foot of the slope to the cliff top. Castlemartin peninsula came to the attention of the War Department in 1939, and the old storage magazines and some of the rails from that time are visible in the St Govan's Head area. After some fifty years as a Royal Armoured Corps range Castlemartin Range is now a field training centre for the Army. There are guided walks along the coast through the Range from Stack Rocks to Freshwater West, but given the extraordinary beauty and importance of the limestone cliffs they seem all too rare.

WALK DIRECTIONS [-] indicates history note

1. Starting from the St Govan's Inn in Bosherston [1] head towards the church and the car park to it's right. Take the path leading downhill to the lily ponds. At the first lily pond take the path bearing left and cross the footbridge.

2. Continue on the path leading around the pond to cross a second footbridge. The path from here ascends to meet a track. Bear right [2].

3. The path descends to a third footbridge. Turn right and cross the bridge. Continue on the sandy path, keeping to the pond edge, to reach the junction of the lily ponds and Broad Haven.

4. Cross the wooden footbridge to gain Broad Haven beach [3]. Keeping the outlet stream to your left cross the beach in front of the sand dunes to gain Broad Haven car park. Steps will lead you up from the beach to the car park.

5. Turn left at the top of the path and cross the car park to a wooden stile leading into a field.

6. Cross the field to Castlemartin Range entrance stile and gate. There is a Range hut, with warning notices clearly displayed. If there are red flags flying do not cross! Assuming all is well cross the Range. The path route is marked by white posts – and there are plenty of signs marked *Danger – Military Firing Range – Keep Out* to keep you on the path. A safe stroll through the gorse, with (in winter at least) plenty of sheep for company.

7. Where the Range path joins the tarmac road leading to the Coastguard lookout there is the option to detour left to the lookout, or continue right, crossing by a cattle grid, to immediately gain the access point to St Govan's chapel [4] and the car park.

8. The route down to St Govan's chapel is indicated by a six pointed star. Some seventy four steps will lead you down – though legend has it that it is impossible to count the same number of steps going back up as were counted on the way down!

9. Return to Bosherston and the starting point along the tarmac road leading inland away from the chapel and car park. The road passes Royal Navy Control Tower Newton, and a smaller Range hut, also Newton, both on the left hand side.

FACILITIES

Pub, public toilets, and BT telephone in Bosherston. Also a seasonal café – Ye Olde Worlde Café, and a Coastguard station (occasionally manned). Public toilets at Broad Haven car park. Emergency telephones at St Govan's Head (Coastguard lookout) and St Govan's chapel Range entrance. Coarse fishing permits are available from Ye Olde Worlde Café, and National Trust office at Stackpole.

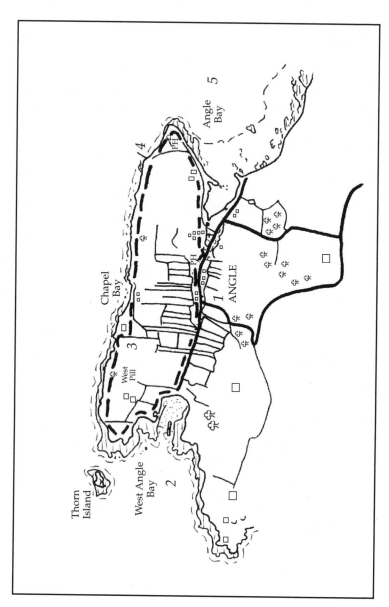

Thorn
Island

West Angle
Bay

2

West
Pill

3

Chapel
Bay

PH

ANGLE

1

PH

4

PH

Angle
Bay

5

6. angle

3.75 miles/6 kilometres

Note: Make the most of the Angle peninsula by utilising the footpath leading inland from just before Freshwater West at Gravel Bay to make a proper thirst quencher of a walk – 9.5 miles / 15.5 kilometres.

OS Maps: OS 1:25 000 South Pembrokeshire Outdoor Leisure 36.
Start: The Old Point House.
Access: Angle is reached on the B4320 from Pembroke, or via Castlemartin on the B4319. The Old Point House overlooks Angle Bay, and can be reached from the unmetalled road leading off right from the main road through Angle, shortly after entering the village, and just before the church. Signposted. Bus routes 364 and 387/388 Pembroke Dock – Stackpole – Angle.
Parking: At the Old Point House car park. Parking also possible outside the Hibernia, and at the free car park at West Angle Bay. Note – at high tides the road to the Point House is under water for a short time!
Grade: Easy.

The Old Point House (01646 641205)
Enjoying one of the finest views of any Pembrokeshire inn the building itself dates back to 1700, it's documented history as a pub dating from the early 19th century. Well favoured over the years by a succession of Angle's lifeboat crews it is a popular place, particularly during the summer months where it is easy to while away an afternoon watching the boats come and go in Angle Bay.

Hibernia Inn (01646 641517)
Hibernia is the old Latin name for Ireland, and one explanation for the name being applied to the inn was the finding of an old

Irish coin during building work on the pub, the coin itself being dated to 1805, and a replica on display in the entrance hall. The inn itself was opened in about 1865, possibly to cash in on trade generated by the building of the fort on Thorn island. Closed in 1971 it re-opened in 1979.

HISTORY NOTES
1. Angle
Angle's long main street, with it's flat roofed houses, colonnaded former hotel, and scattered medieval buildings, has a distinctiveness unique in Pembrokeshire. Taking it's name from it's geographical position, in an 'angle' of land, the village grew up around it's Norman landowners. Alongside the growing village were the strip fields which helped supply the Norman manor with food. These medieval strip fields are still there, and retain their original shape, stretched out as they are behind the houses on either side of the main street. The only difference now is that they are enclosed. Just north of the church is a 14th century sandstone tower house. Similar to tower houses in Ireland, Angle's tower house is unique in Wales. Above a vaulted undercroft are three storeys which would have been the living quarters. Access would have been at first floor level, thus allowing the occupants to seal themselves in should they be attacked. It was possibly the residence of the de Shirburn family, who were Lords of the Manor here from the late 13th to the 15th centuries. There is public access. A short distance

Angle's tower house

74

away, on private land, is a dovecote which would have provided plump pigeon pie for the table.

The church, dedicated to St Mary the Virgin, is 13th century, or at least the north wall and north transept are, the church was much restored in the 1850s. The tower is 15th century. There is a fishermen's chapel in the grounds. Dedicated to St Anthony it was built by Edward de Shirburn in 1447. There is also a tiered preaching, or Calvary cross, by the church entrance. Such crosses consist of a Latin cross mounted on three steps, symbolising Charity, Hope, and at the top, Faith. Just south of the main street, by the Post Office, is another medieval building. Marked as a fortified dwelling on OS maps there has been speculation that it may have been a nunnery. Certainly pilgrims sailed from West Angle Bay to Ireland, and across the Haven, near Dale, is Monk Haven, where pilgrims landed en route to St David's. Angle's distinctive flat roofed houses were built or restored at the end of the 19th century by the then owner of the Angle estate to remind him of the building style he had encountered on a tour of duty in South Africa. Nowadays Angle is very much a residential village, with some second homes.

2. West Angle Bay

West Angle Bay is pleasant and attractive, with lots of sand, and plenty of rock pools for the young explorer. Situated as it is at the mouth of the Haven it has always played a part in it's defence. Following the scares of the Spanish Armada in 1588 Henry VIII had two defensive towers built, one, partly extant, on the eastern headland overlooking West Angle, the other, now vanished, on the opposite shore near St Ann's Head. Further 19th century fears, this time of French invasion, led to the establishment of an extensive system of defensible barracks and blockhouses. Often known as Palmerston's Follies, after the Prime Minister and Foreign Secretary of the time, there was a blockhouse, of which the gun emplacements remain, on the eastern headland, by Henry VIII's tower, and another on Thorn island. Since the 1930s Thorn island's grey eminence has,

West Angle Bay

though not at present, made a fine isolated hotel. During the Second World War Angle airfield was home to both spitfires and hurricanes. Operational from June 1941 to early 1943 there is a memorial plaque in the car park. Recent archaeological excavations on the headland to the left of the bay have revealed the presence of an early Christian burial ground, probably 9th or 10th century. It is believed a church dedicated to St Anthony once stood here.

Angle Brickworks flourished here from the 1870s, one of perhaps a dozen or so in the county. Producing bricks, tiles, and drain pipes, all that now remains is the brick chimney, behind the present cafe. To the right of the beach, just past the lime kiln, is an old limestone quarry. Providing stone for Thorn island, and lime for the brickworks and the land, there was at one time a tramway connecting quarry and brickworks, along the route taken by the present Coast Path. A passage blasted out on the seaward side has made it a sheltered harbour. There have always been wrecks around this dangerous coast; one of the most famous being the *Loch Shiel*, en route from Glasgow to

Adelaide Australia, with seven thousand cases of whiskey. Wrecked on Thorn island in 1894 the crew were successfully rescued by the Angle lifeboat; however only two thousand of the whiskey cases were officially recovered. Angle people are a hardy race! One recent disaster was the oil tanker *Sea Empress*, holed on the Mid Channel rocks at the entrance to the Haven in February 1996, leaking seventy thousand tons of crude oil into the sea in the process. All visible traces of the oil spill were soon virtually eradicated from the local beaches, and the decline in the number of seabirds immediately after the spill proved to be temporary. More long-lived species, like the shore lichens, are taking longer to recover.

3. Chapel Bay fort

Built in 1890, and part of the haven's 19th century defences, there was a fort here at Chapel Bay, complete with an inland moat. The fort is currently the subject of a renovation project, with the ultimate aim of opening the site to the public. The line of the moat is clearly visible.

4. Angle lifeboat station

There has been a lifeboat at Angle since the 1860s. Originally known as the Milford Haven lifeboat the first station was built at Angle Point; the brick remains are all that are now left. The station moved permanently to it's present position in the 1920s. The current station dates from 1992. A new Tamar class lifeboat is due in 2009, replacing the Tyne class *The Lady Rank.*

5. Angle Bay

The area between Angle, and, across the water, the inlets of Dale and Sandy Haven, is traditionally the best area in the haven for sea fishing, and Angle Bay has provided safe anchorage and shelter for countless fishermen and yachtsmen. The extensive mud flats provide important feeding grounds for wintering ducks and waders. The industrial complex across the bay is Texaco refinery.

WALK DIRECTIONS [-] indicates history note

1. Starting from the Old Point House pub continue along the track leading back to the village [1], and where the track branches left over a bridge go straight ahead.

2. Just past the medieval tower house go through a gate and walk diagonally left to reach a play area. Go through the play area to reach the main road through Angle.

3. Turn right and continue, passing the Hibernia Inn on the right, to West Angle Bay [2].

4. From West Angle Bay follow the track to West Pill farm, shortly branching off to the left onto the Coast Path. Clearly signposted.

5. Continue on the Coast Path, passing opposite Thorn island, and then on past Chapel Bay fort [3] and Angle lifeboat station [4] to reach Angle Point and Angle Bay [5].

6. Continue the short distance to reach the starting point.

FACILITIES

Most facilities available in Angle. BT telephone, public toilets, seasonal café, and caravan park at West Angle Bay. Freshwater West, nearby, has one of the finest beaches and dune systems in the county, complete with renovated hut where edible seaweed was dried before being made into laver bread! Can be a dangerous beach for inexperienced swimmers.

7. carew and milton

2.2 miles/3.5 kilometres

OS Maps: OS 1:25 000 South Pembrokeshire Outdoor Leisure 36.
Start: Carew Inn.
Access: Carew is on the A4075, which itself leads off the A477
Pembroke Dock to Kilgetty and St Clears main road at Milton
roundabout. Bus services 360 Tenby to Carew and Milton and
361 Tenby to Carew and Milton to Pembroke Dock
Parking: Car park opposite Carew Inn adjacent to the castle.
Limited parking in the pub car park. Car park also by the mill
pond itself – to reach cross the road bridge and turning left
follow the minor road for a short distance, and limited parking
possible in Milton.
Grade: Easy.

Carew Inn (01646 651267)
Dating from 1868 the inn would seem to have been created from
two adjoining properties, the smaller property now being the
bar. Testifying to the inn's role in the community the inn has
acted at one time, in the mid 19th century, as the meeting place
of the Carew Ivorites Club, a friendly society, and until recently,
was the headquarters of the local cricket and football clubs. Has
a pleasant garden overlooking the castle.

The Milton Brewery Inn (01646 651202)
As it's name suggests it was once a brewery. The local streams
which flow into the Carew river from the nearby Ridgeway (the
ridge that runs across south Pembrokeshire) led to the
establishment of corn and carding mills, and one of the local
millers added malting barley and brewing to his labours in the
1830s. Another member of the same family operated a malt
house here in the 1840s. A tap house attached to the brewery
was noted in the 1860s, rejoicing in the name of the Bridge End;
however this soon became changed to the Milton Brewery inn.

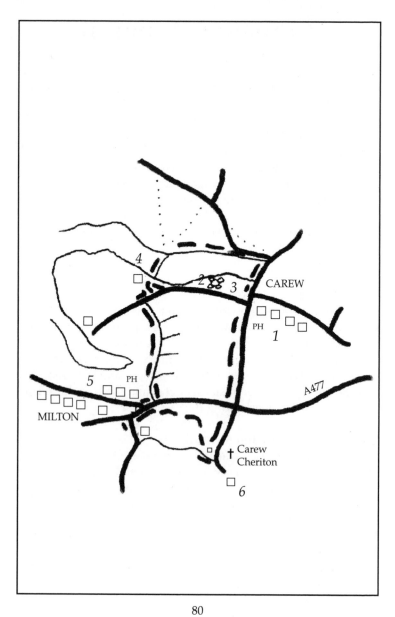

CAREW

PH

A477

MILTON

Carew
Cheriton

1

2 3

4

5

6

For a short time aerated water was also manufactured and sold, but by 1910 brewing had ceased. The well which supplied the water has now been covered over, and is currently under the pool table. A local tale has it that the house opposite the main entrance had a much higher wall adjacent to the village road at one time in it's history. Once the Three Horsehoes it's landlord had originally built it higher so that Milton Brewery could not be seen from the main road!

HISTORY NOTES
1. Carew Village
Like many other villages in the shade of a castle Carew's origins and prosperity would have grown with the history of the castle. Traders and craftsmen would have settled to help serve the castle and it's lord. There is a renovated medieval conical round chimney on the road into the village, just past the pub, though the house to which it once belonged has long disappeared. The name Carew may derive from the Welsh Caerau, meaning forts – there are ancient prehistoric burial mounds in the area.

2. Carew Castle
Carew castle, in it's glorious strategic setting, is one of Wales' finest. It is believed to have been founded by Gerald de Windsor, castellan of Pembroke from 1093 to 1116. There were various additions over the centuries until circa 1480 Gerald's descendants sold it to Sir Rhys ap Thomas who enhanced the building, and is famed as the giver, in 1507, of the last great medieval tournament of Britain. Five days of feasting, harp music, and song were accompanied by contests of tilting, athletics, wrestling and deer hunting in the park,

Carew 500

with evenings of theatricals and drinking. It is said a thousand men attended, and not a single fight or quarrel broke out! Five hundred years later May 2007 saw a re-enactment of the Great Tournament, with six days of concerts, medieval story telling, archery, falconry and hunting displays culminating in the Great Joust, with knights in full armour on horseback fighting lance to lance for the prize of champion.

On the impeachment of Sir Rhys' grandson the castle passed to Sir John Perrott, reputedly the son of Henry VIII. Lord Deputy of Ireland, and a Privy Councillor, he continued the castle's transformation into a brilliant Elizabethan palace, adding the superb North Gallery with it's mullioned windows. Turkish carpets, Irish rugs, silks, books and musical instruments and piped water were added to the interior. However before he could occupy it he was convicted of treason, and died in the Tower of London in 1592. After this great flowering the castle

Carew Inn and Celtic Cross

fell on hard times, suffering two sieges during the Civil War before falling into ruin. The castle is now open to the public Easter to October.

3. Carew Cross

Carew's magnificent Celtic Christian cross can be dated to 1035. It is a royal memorial to Maredudd, who with his brother Hywel, became joint ruler of Deheubarth (now south west Wales) in 1033. Maredudd was killed in 1035. The inscription to him recorded on the front of the cross (facing the castle) reads MARGIT EUT REX ETG FILIUS – [The cross of] Maredudd (Magriteut) son of Edwin. It was moved to it's present position early in the 20th century; originally it was on a outcrop projecting into the road.

4. Carew Tidal Mill

In days gone by, when Carew French tidal mill was flourishing (French because it is believed French burr stones were used), steam barges and wooden sailing ships would have been seen heading up to the mill to deliver corn from Sandy Haven and other Milford Haven creeks, perhaps even from Bristol. The ground seed would have found local use. Nowadays the wide and shallow Carew river, home to curlew and shelduck, is only likely to play host to the occasional adventurous dinghy. There has been a mill upriver here since at least 1542, the present building dating probably from the early 19th century. The revival in agriculture of the late 18th century restored the fortunes of the mill, however by 1937 operation had ceased. The earliest reference to the causeway itself dates from 1630, when it was noted that repairs had been made to it earlier in that century. Since restoration in 1972 Wales' only restored tidal mill can be visited from Easter to October.

5. Milton

Milton, or the mill settlement, dates from at least the 14th century. At it's centre would have been the grist, or corn mill, which continued in operation until the early 20th century – the walk passes by it's remains. The settlement was also involved in the production of textiles as there were also two carding mills in the vicinity, their historical presence noted both in Tudor times and in the 19th century. The distinctive red building visible from the walkway was the former waterworks and pumping station. Built in 1898 to supply south Pembrokeshire it continued in operation until circa 1970.

6. Carew Church

Earliest reference to the church dates from 1203, with the present chancel and transepts dating from 1326. It is an impressive building, with it's corner steeple it's most obvious distinction. The high altar was erected by public subscription to local men who fell during the 1914-18 war, the font, said to be an exact copy of an earlier Norman one, dates from the mid 19th century. The tower itself dates from just after 1500, however it needed repair after it was struck by lightning in 1926, costing an impressive, for the time, £1900. Effigies in the church include one of the Carew family in armour, and dated to the late 13th/early 14th century. The church is dedicated to St Mary. The chantry chapel in the grounds, adjacent to the church path, was once used as a school, and a home for paupers. The church cemetery has war graves for those who were killed whilst serving at RAF Carew Cheriton during the 2nd World War, when Carew had it's own airfield.

WALK DIRECTIONS [-] indicates history note

1. Starting from Carew [1] Inn and village walk down the hill past the castle [2] and Celtic cross [3] to reach the river and millpond, and after crossing the bridge turn left to reach the car park by the millpond.

2. Continue on the path alongside the pond, and cross the causeway left to reach the tidal mill [4]. Take the metal road leading away from the mill, to shortly turn right onto another metalled track. After a short distance cross a stone stile on your left.

3. Keeping to the left continue across fields to cross another

stone stile on the left to enter a field. Bear right along the field edge to reach the main road.

4. Turn right at the main road and continue on a path and crossing Milton's 1820 road bridge reach Milton [5] – Milton Brewery on right. Cross the main road and take the minor road opposite.

5. Just past the farm shop on the left turn left across a wooden footbridge and continue on a metal path, passing the ruins of Milton mill on your left, and finally as the path bears right reach a minor road. Bear left and continue into Carew Cheriton and Carew church [6]. Once at the village bear left.

6. Continue on the minor road, again cross the main road, and keeping ahead return to the starting point.

FACILITIES

Public toilets in Carew village, near the pub. Disused Carew airfield nearby has a Sunday market, and the recently restored Control Tower can be visited Sundays in July and August, and on Bank holidays. The Sealed Knot, the Civil War re-enactment society, hold events during the year in the castle grounds.

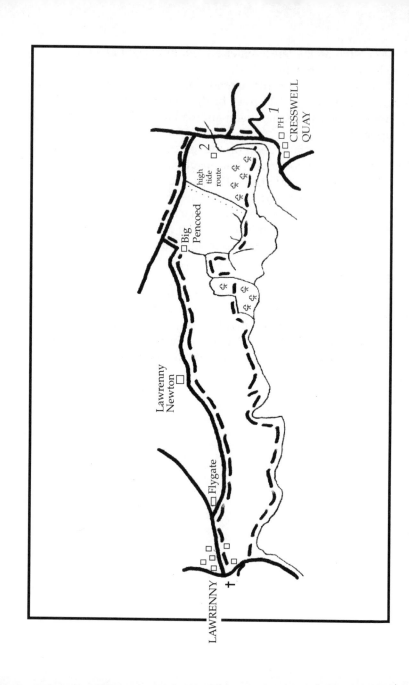

8. cResswell quay

5.5 miles/8.75 kilometres

Note: The stepping stones at Cresswell Quay can only be crossed at low tide. High tide alternative noted under walk directions. Link with Lawrenny and Landshipping walks to make a full day by the river.

OS Maps: OS 1:25 000 South Pembrokeshire Outdoor Leisure 36.
Start: Cresselly Arms.
Access: Cresswell Quay is by the Cresswell river on the minor road leading off from the A4075 Canaston Bridge road at Cresselly. Bus 361 Pembroke Dock to Tenby stops at Cresswell Quay.
Parking: By the Cresselly Arms.
Grade: Moderate.

Cresselly Arms (016464 651202)
This at least two hundred years old pub began life as the Quay and Compass. Originally a beer house it was upgraded to a pub in 1872, with a change of name to the Quay Head, though it soon reverted to the Quay and Compass. In 1892 the local squire decided the Cresselly estate, of which the Quay and Compass formed a part, needed a proper hostelry, both for locals and hunt followers, and for visiting tourists. With refurbishment and extra bedrooms the inn became the Cresselly Arms, though it has now long ceased to be an hotel. Part of the pub's attraction is the retention of it's traditional interior, with it's red and black floor tiles and local photographs. There is an open fire (when needed) in one room, and an aga in another. Beer is tapped straight from the barrel into jug. Another great attraction is the beauty of it's setting – there are seats out by the water, and given it's position on a tidal creek customers can arrive by boat, and often do. Along with it's creeper covered exterior it is one of the finest pubs in the country. The exterior still has the old AA road

sign pinned to it – 237 ¼ miles to London. Occasional sales of second hand books have taken place outside during the warmer months – sales going to cancer research.

HISTORY NOTES
1. Cresswell Quay

Cresswell Quay lies in the boundaries of the Pembrokeshire coalfield, itself an extension of the South Wales coalfield. Mining in Pembrokeshire was never as sophisticated as in South Wales, and remained rural in character, but it was profitable enough to provide work and income for many over a considerable period of time; certainly it has been part of Pembrokeshire's industrial fabric since the 14th century, with it's slow decline dating from the 19th century. Most of the coal mining areas came under the ownership of a relatively small number of landowners who more often than not would lease out the mining rights to

Cresselly Arms

entrepreneurs who would then employ miners and tradesmen to work the colliery. A colliery itself might comprise a number of small coal pits spread out over a locality – it is estimated that within the local parishes of Loveston, Jeffreston, Carew and Reynalton over fifty pits or groups of pits have been recorded between the years 1768 to 1828.

Pembrokeshire produces fine anthracite, but in much smaller quantities than the less valued culm, which was used locally for lime burning (lime being needed for Pembrokeshire's acid soils) and domestic usage. Once brought to the surface the coal needed to reach market as soon as possible, and Pembrokeshire's creeks and rivers provided a natural means of transport. Dating from the first half of the 18th century a coal fold was built at Cresswell to hold coal and culm (also timber) from pits within five or six miles distance; it's ruins are those on the opposite side of the river from the Cresselly Arms, reached across the stepping stones. Access then was by cart across a ford, more or less where the present stepping stones lie. The small roofless building in the corner of the fold, adjacent to the river, may have been the counting house, weigh house or office.

Once stored the coal needed to be shipped, and existing quays were utilised, or built to assist. Again local landowners had part ownership of the quays as with the mines, and had control over the barges and small ships that carried the coal downriver. Here at Cresswell coal was transshipped to Lawrenny for loading onto larger vessels. Three quays can still be seen at Cresswell. Most obvious is the one in front of the pub, however this seems to have been used more for general goods; it's probable last commercial use was in December 1948 to receive a shipment of culm from Hook, sited further up on the Western Cleddau river. The other two are opposite each other, one in front of the coal fold mirrored by one on the opposite bank, though neither are in great condition! In truth Cresswell Quay's industrial heyday was probably over by the mid 1830s, and it's industrial buildings and coal quays have been in detioration ever since.

2. Cresswell Castle and Bridge

Cresswell castle, so marked on the OS map, was in reality before it's present ruined state more a mansion, and built as such in imitation of the earlier more robust and necessary defensible structures required by the Norman occupiers of Wales. Believed to have been built by William Barlow, Bishop of St David's from 1536 to 1548, it later passed to his brother Roger Barlow of Slebech, and continued in occupation through various branches of the family, probably until the late 18th century. A distinctive feature of the mansion was it's four corner towers, one of which featured as a dovecote, pigeons being a popular source of medieval food. It's towers can still be picked out quite clearly. Near to the ruined mansion are the remains of a chapel and a holy well. Cresswell bridge may be contemporary with the mansion. It was probably rebuilt in the early 18th century when adopted as a county bridge, it's carriageway raised and the parapets rebuilt. A distinctive feature are the stone steps leading down from it to the river bank. Just passed the bridge is the old renovated water corn mill, now a holiday cottage complex.

WALK DIRECTIONS [-] indicates history note

1. Starting from Cresswell Quay [1] cross the Cresswell river by the stepping stones situated to the right of the Cresselly Arms, and once across and keeping the industrial ruins to your left, ascend through Scotland Wood to meet a concrete farm track and the high tide route.

2. Those requiring the high ride route from Cresswell Quay will find it by walking along the minor road from Cresswell Quay towards Lawrenny, crossing Cresswell Bridge, and continuing left on the minor road to Lawrenny to turn off onto a concreted farm track through a metal gate to meet the track leading up from the stepping stones route. Distance to the farm gate from Cresswell Quay just over half a mile/three quarters of a kilometre.

3. If ascending from the river through Scotland Wood cross the farm track, or if walking the high tide route where the concrete path ends at a field turn right, and continue on a path/green lane to fields.

4. Keeping to the field edges, initially right then left, the route soon ascends steps to reach an open field above Tanyard Mountain – the OS map has the route going through woodland here; however this is an error (at least on my edition), instead keep to the edge of the open field to meet a track giving access to Tanyard Mountain.

5. Bear left onto the track, and then crossing a stile bear right and continue keeping field boundaries to your left for some 1.5 miles/2.5 kilometres. At a three way sign post and metal gate (the second after Lawrenny church tower comes into view) bear left over a boardwalk, and crossing a stone stile reach the minor road into Lawrenny.

6. Bear right into Lawrenny village, and again right to take the road leading out of Lawrenny. Take the first minor road on the right at Flygate and continue through Lawrenny Newton until at Big Pencoed farm the road bears left to join the minor road from Lawrenny to Cresswell Quay. Bear right, and continuing right, cross Cresswell bridge [2], to reach the starting point.

FACILITIES

Post Office and shop at Lawrenny. Toilets at Cresswell Quay and public telephone at Lawrenny and Cresswell Quay. Penquoit Centre by turning to Big Pencoed farm.

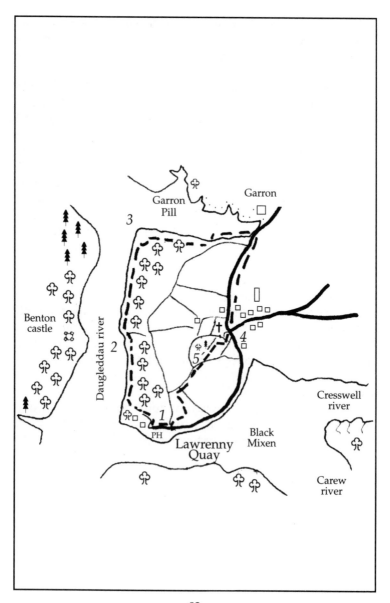

Garron
Garron
Pill

3

Benton
castle

Daugleddau river

2

1

PH

Lawrenny
Quay

Black
Mixen

Cresswell
river

Carew
river

4

5

9. Lawrenny

3 miles/4.75 kilometres

Note: The section along Garron Pill includes shore walking – check your tide tables as the shore will be under water at high tide! Walk can be linked with the Landshipping walk via the footpath alongside Garron pill, and/or combine with the route to Cresswell Quay.

OS Maps: OS 1:25 000 South Pembrokeshire Outdoor Leisure 36.
Start: Lawrenny Arms.
Access: Lawrenny can be reached from the A4075 Carew to Canaston Bridge road, either following the minor road from Cresselly, or from Cross Hands near Oakwood Theme Park. Just follow the Lawrenny signposts. Occasional bus service Tuesdays and Fridays – check with Information Centres for details.
Parking: Car park at Lawrenny Arms or in the parking bay at the Yacht station. Parking also possible in Lawrenny village.
Grade: Easy.

Lawrenny Arms (01646 651439)
At one time, in the late 18th century, the parish boasted seven pubs, but now the Lawrenny Arms is the only one in the immediate vicinity. One mid 19th century local squire, with a keen interest in hunting, developed the properties here into kennels and houses for the huntsman and kennelman. One hundred years later further development saw the birth of the Kirkland Arms – Kirkland being a local racehorse which won the Grand National back in 1905. This later became the Lawrenny Arms, though in memory of it's history it often gets referred to as the Doghouse!

HISTORY NOTES

1. Lawrenny Quay

For centuries the sea and inland rivers have served as a magical highway for Pembrokeshire trade, commerce and communication. Viking raiders penetrated the Milford Haven as far north as Haverfordwest, whilst embattled Normans took care wherever possible to build their castles not only on strategic sites, but also on sites that overlooked or had access to the waterways of the Haven and the Daugleddau. From the Middle Ages onwards cargoes of coal, limestone, timber and grain set out from and arrived at all ports of call on the river. In this atmosphere of bustle and activity Lawrenny's prosperity grew; it's quay was developed, and it's shipbuilding industry increased in importance.

At nearby West Williamston, across the water at the junction of the Carew and Cresswell rivers, channels had been cut to give barges of fifteen to twenty tons access to it's limestone quarries. Often the barges carried their loads to Haverfordwest, but it was usual to transship them at Lawrenny. A significant coal measure extended in a narrow strip from Saundersfoot to Nolton, passing to the north of Lawrenny. Those collieries of the Daugleddau Coalfield adjacent to the river established small quays for export. When visiting ships outgrew these quays, as they did at Cresswell and Landshipping, it became customary for barges to take the coal to Lawrenny, or nearby Llangwm, for reloading into waiting ships. It was for this purpose that Lawrenny's quay had been developed. People, as well as cargoes, were constantly on the move from Lawrenny Quay. Ferries took people and their wares down to Cosheston ferry and across to Roose ferry. The last ferry service continued until the 1960s.

At one time Lawrenny's shipyard was second only to Milford Haven's. From the 1800s through to the 1850s Milford built 91 ships; whilst Lawrenny's total was 61. The building of new towns downriver; Milford Haven from the 1790s,

Lawrenny Quay

Pembroke Dock from 1814, and Neyland as the railway terminus from 1856, together with larger ships, spelt the end of village trade and quays. There was no shipbuilding at Lawrenny after the 1850s. Lawrenny Quay now is a pleasant holiday site, catering to the boating and walking enthusiast, as well as the day tripper.

2. The Daugelddau and Benton Castle

The Daugleddau (the two swords) is strictly speaking that part of the river from the Cleddau Bridge to Picton Point, where the western and eastern sections of the river join. The Daugleddau, with it's many small creeks, or pills, are a series of drowned river valleys, or rias, formed at the end of the Ice Age. The woodland is semi-natural oak, with the occasional wild service tree. Deciduous woodlands are now a rarity in Pembrokeshire and are found mainly here, on the banks of the Daugleddau, or further north in the Gwaun valley, near Fishguard. Steep valley slopes have been their best defence against farming. Benton castle, opposite, with it's smart coat of whitewash, dates from the 13th century, reputedly built by Bishop Beck of St David's. Substantially rebuilt in the 1930s, it is now a private residence.

3. Garron Pill

Garron pill is typical of the many small inlets on the river. From here the river's pattern of alternating low meadow land and steep wooded slopes abutting the shore becomes evident. The mudflats provide good feeding grounds for wildfowl and waders. Curlews, shelduck and teal compete with widgeon and mallard. The town of Llangwm, diagonally opposite, was famous in the 19th century for the quality of it's oysters. There have been recent attempts here to revive the industry by farming oyster beds on pontoons. These are set at the mouth of the pill, allowing for access at low tide. The women of Llangwm were noted in the county and South Wales for their individualism. At one time they used to row their menfolk downriver to work at the new towns, returning later in the day to collect them. They had their own distinctive fashion, and travelled from town to village selling the local fish and oysters. The wooden hut, overlooking the pill, is used by the local scouts and guides.

4. Lawrenny Church

Lawrenny's fine church is the only one in the county dedicated to the 12th century Celtic saint Caradoc, who is known to have lived in Pembrokeshire. Originally late 13th century, a west tower was added in the 16th century. There are hand held information panels inside the church, which is well worth a visit.

5. Site of Lawrenny Castle

Stunning views over Black Mixen below and the Carew and Cresswell rivers. The old limestone quarries at West Williamston opposite are now managed as a nature reserve. There have been two mansions here on this site. Early 18th century Lawrenny House was demolished to make way for Lawrenny castle, a magnificent Victorian house dating from 1850, sadly demolished in the 1950s after failures to find a buyer.

The castle became the officer's mess during the Second World War when the Navy arrived with a seaplane training squadron in 1941. Lawrenny soon echoed to the sounds of Kingfisher and Walrus seaplane engines.

WALK DIRECTIONS [-] indicates history note

1. Start from the Lawrenny Arms in Lawrenny Quay [1]. Continue on the road to the boat park. Cross to gain a woodland path.

2 Continue on the woodland track until, after a short distance, you reach a private house. Bear right and continue. There are fine views of the river and Benton castle opposite [2], before the path turns right inland by Garron pill [3].

3. Continue on the woodland path, passing the scout/guides hut, to reach a stile on your left. Cross the stile and follow the steps down to the shore. Turn right and continue inland along the shore.

4. At the minor road turn right and continue uphill to Lawrenny village.

5. Walk past the church entrance [4] and enter fields through a metal gate. Continue ahead, initially alongside a stone wall. Where the wall ends bear right uphill to reach a second metal gate.

6. Bear left and continue ahead, keeping the crenellated wall to your right. Above is the site of the now demolished Lawrenny castle [5]. Keep ahead until the path bears left downhill through woodland to join the minor road opposite the Lawrenny Arms.

FACILITIES

The public toilets opposite the Lawrenny Arms are open April to October only. BT telephone opposite the Yacht station. Quayside tearoom. Lawrenny village has a Post Office/shop and BT telephone. Slipway at Lawrenny Yacht Station, which keeps some of it's moorings for visitors. Also caters for boat engine repairs. Youth Hostel in Lawrenny village.

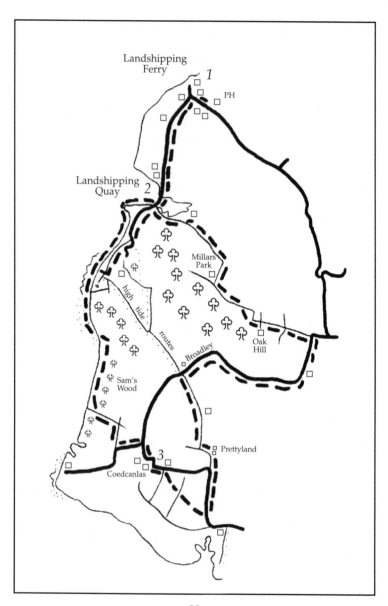

Landshipping
Ferry

1

PH

Landshipping
Quay

2

Millars
Park

high tide
routes

Oak
Hill

Broadley

Sam's
Wood

Prettyland

3

Coedcanlas

10. Landshipping

6 miles/9.5 kilometres

Note: The section from Landshipping Quay to Sam's Wood includes shore walking – check your tide tables as the shore will be under water at high tide! There are high tide alternatives noted in the walk directions for this section. The walk can be combined with those for Lawrenny and Cresswell Quay to make a good long distance pub crawl.

OS Maps: OS 1:25 000 South Pembrokeshire Outdoor Leisure 36.
Start: Stanley Arms in Landshipping Ferry.
Access: Landshipping can be reached on minor roads from the A4075 Canaston Bridge to Carew road. Quickest access from Cross Hands, near Oakwood Theme Park. Occasional bus service Tuesdays and Fridays – check with Information Centres for details.
Parking: Car parking also possible at Landshipping Quay.
Grade: Moderate.

The Stanley Arms (01834 891424)
The Stanley Arms started life as the Landshipping Inn. Built and owned by a leading family of the time the Owens also built the now ruined Landshipping House by the slipway. Debts due to electioneering forced sale of the inn, among other assets, in 1857, and sales particulars noted the outbuildings as including a dairy, piggery, stable and brewhouse, and 32 acres, the tenant combining his trade with farming. The inn was the centre of local life, many of those who were later to be killed in the Garden Pit mining disaster belonged to a Lodge of Odd Fellows who met at the inn from 1842 onwards. The Landshipping estate, including the inn, was bought by a Major Stanley of Brighton, the inn remaining in the Stanley family hands until 1922 when it was sold to a Hugh Thomas from Milford Haven, the sales particulars now including dairy, bakehouse, pigsties,

stable and cowshed, and 59 acres – by this time the inn had also been acting as the village shop and post office. The name change to the Stanley Arms took place in 1910. After the death of Hugh Thomas ownership passed to the Allen family, William Allen holding the tenancy from 1918. In response to increases in tourism the inn was expanded in the 1960s, and has remained popular with both locals and visitors. The inn has again been recently resold. The bar has an attractive slate floor, and there is a restaurant area and garden.

HISTORY NOTES
1. Landshipping Ferry
Now isolated Landshipping was once part of an almost forgotten Pembrokeshire transport system that linked road to road and village to village by the use of local ferries across the county's inland rivers. In it's heyday a ferry linked Landshipping with the Picton side on the opposite shore. By the early 20th century a bus service had been introduced to take passengers on from Picton to the Rhos and to Haverfordwest for shopping and visiting. The cost to use the ferry at this time was threepence; those who brought their bicycle had to fork out an extra sixpence. The ferry remained in operation until the 1930s. There was also a once weekly steamer to Pembroke Dock and it's market. The shell of Landshipping House still stands on private land by the slipway, last used as a residence in the early 19th century.
2. Landshipping Quay
The name Landshipping suggests a link with the water, however it derives from *long shippen*, or cowshed, a much more down to earth explanation. Landshipping's industrial heyday was though much more to do with it's position in the Daugleddau coalfield, and the exploitation of the coal seams that underlay the area, it's rewards adding economic supplement to the agricultural mainstay. Pembrokeshire's anthracite was in much demand, and was shipped out down

river from the many local pits to Lawrenny Quay for onward transshipment to London and export to Europe. Whilst early 19th century saw vessels sailing up river to Landshipping it became the norm to load onto barges. A new quay was constructed at Landshipping in 1800, with the addition of a tramroad the following year. Whilst many of the pits in Pembrokeshire's coalfield were small, and ownership under the control of a number of different owners, by the late 18th century Landshipping's collieries were under the ownership of the Owens of Orielton. This concentration of ownership offered greater economic prospects and in 1800 the first steam engine to be used in a Pembrokeshire coalfield was installed, the same year the new quay was constructed. Cost was £1,900. 1801 saw an immediate improvement with the export of 10,912 tons of coal.

Prior to the 1844 there were some five collieries in operation, but disaster struck on February 14th 1844 when the tide broke into the working of the Garden Pit colliery, which extended out under the river. Of the fifty eight miners at work only eighteen returned to the surface. The forty dead included men, women and children; the youngest being nine years of age. The memorial at the Quay was erected in 2002 – it is thought that those prefaced by Miner in their name were women; both the employment of women and boys under ten years of age had been banned by Act of Parliament two years previously. Mining did not end immediately, however by the late 1860s production at all the local collieries had ceased, and population decline set in. Quays were left to fall into ruin, and the cottages and houses that once housed the colliery workers, together with shops and public houses that served them, were left to either disappear from the landscape, or find new uses.

One legacy left to the area was the introduction of the difficult art of compass fishing by two Gloucestershire men, Ormond and Edwards, who worked in the Landshipping colliery in the 18th century. A technique suited to fast flowing

Daugleddau river and Garron pill

rivers a boat is held stationery in mid stream by means of ropes secured to stakes driven into the mud banks ashore. Held taut by two poles a V shaped net is then positioned vertically beneath the boat's keel, the two poles resting on the river bed. Fishing is possible for only three hours or so after the beginning of the ebb tide. At one time some hundred or so fishermen from nearby Llangwm and Hook made a commercial living during the 19th century from this method, hauling in salmon, sewin and bass, but nowadays a compass fisherman is a rare sight.

3. Coedcanlas

Coedcanlas has a rich history. There was a manor house here in medieval times, the manor passing to the ownership of the Owens of Orielton in the 17th century. They set about establishing a Renaissance style garden. There would have been orchards and lawns running down to the river, with a hop garden, stone lined pond with stream, and vegetable beds. The front door of the house would have faced down river. Nowadays the garden has long gone, though it's traces can be picked out in aerial photographs. The name Coedcanlas probably derives from *Coed Cynlas*, Cynlas' wood. Another distinction is that Coedcanlas was the birthplace of Dick Francis, the author and jockey.

WALK DIRECTIONS [-] indicates history note

1. Starting from the Stanley Arms at Landshipping Ferry [1] walk down the minor road for just over half a mile/ three quarters of a kilometre to Landshipping Quay [2] . It is possible to walk along the foreshore to the Quay at low tides – similar distance. Good views en route of Picton Point on the other side of the river, where the Daugelddau breaks up into the western and eastern Cleddaus.

2. Once at the Quay continue ahead, either along the foreshore or along the road. If taking the road route continue towards Woodhouse to bear right through a farm gate to gain the track leading to Brickyard. Route well signposted. Once at a second gate leading to Brickyard ahead you will need to bear right across a stile to gain the foreshore and join the foreshore route. If the foreshore is flooded there is a high tide alternative here, across a second stile just ahead, the route leading off uphill to Broadley.

3. Whichever route has been chosen continue ahead from this point along the foreshore a short distance to turn left into Sam's Wood through a gate and by a waymarked post. Continue uphill to reach a gate post and then turn right and continue along the path to eventually enter a field at a stile.

4. Go ahead and right, keeping to the left field edge, to reach a stile giving access to a minor road. Continue ahead on the road to reach a T junction. Bear right and just past Coedcanlas [3], opposite a private house named Beggars Reach, bear right through a metal gate and cross diagonally across the field to reach a minor road. If you find yourself at a stile giving access to a field only then you need to bear back left to the road stile, a little way above.

5. Bear left and continue ahead on the road and then on a track to reach Prettyland. Bear left onto a track, and at a gate bear right and keeping to the right edge join the track to Newton, continuing ahead on it to reach a road.

6. Bear right and go ahead for nearly a mile/one and a half kilometres to reach the turning to Oak Hill at the second right angled bend. Continue towards Oak Hill by stile and gate, and keeping to the right hand edge pass Oak Hill on your left to enter a field at a stile and bear right to reach another stile by a gate.

7. Cross the stile and bear left – fine views ahead of Picton castle across the river. Continue keeping to the left field edge to reach a track by houses. Bear right onto the track and passing Millars Park reach the minor road at Landshipping Quay. Bear right to reach the starting point.

FACILITIES

Slipway at Landshipping Ferry.

11. Lampeter Vale

6 miles/9.5 kilometres

Note: Lampeter Vale refers to the valley formed by the river Marlais between Llanddewi Velfrey and Lampeter Velfrey.

OS Maps: OS 1:25 000 South Pembrokeshire Outdoor Leisure 36.
Start: Parc y Lan Inn, Llanddewi Velfrey.
Access: Llanddewi Velfrey is on the main A40. Narberth railway station is close by. Bus service 322 Haverfordwest to Carmarthen – bus stops by the inn.
Parking: Limited parking outside the inn. There is also parking available, just a short distance on from Parc Y Lan inn in the direction of Haverfordwest, on the road access bay in front of houses on the left.
Grade: Moderate.

Parc y Lan Inn (01834 869411)
With the development of Llanddewi Velfrey, and the growth in traffic along the Whitland road, there were built a number of inns to serve travellers. The busy Commercial pub at one time lent it's name to the developing settlement, however with closure in the 1850s it's licence was transferred to the present Parc y Lan Inn. Built on over the years the original pub comprised the present restaurant. The inn is now the only pub in the immediate area. It's name translates as the inn at the top of meadow.

HISTORY NOTES
1. Llanddewi Velfrey
The development of the settlement of Llanddewi Velfrey owes much to it's position on what is now the main A40, the main period of expansion dating from the late 18th and early 19th centuries when the road was under the control of the Whitland Turnpike Trust. In earlier times the ridge route between Henllan

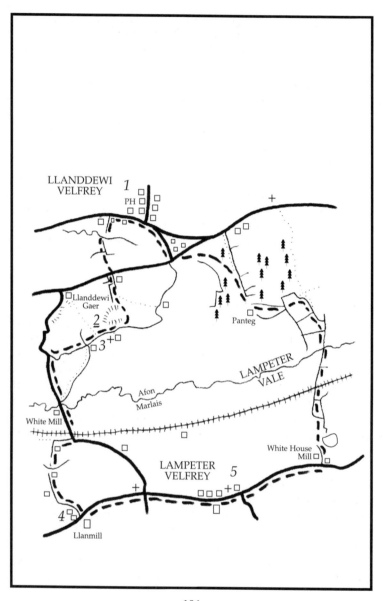

LLANDDEWI
VELFREY *1*

PH

+

Llanddewi
Gaer

2

3 +

Panteg

LAMPETER
VALE

Afon
Marlais

White Mill

White House
Mill

LAMPETER
VELFREY *5*

+

4

Llanmill

and Scapin farm, which the walk crosses, would have been of more importance for it's strategic position. Drovers no doubt would have used this route, and the paths running down it's slopes, to avoid the turnpike toll gates on the main Whitland and, to the south, Tavernspite roads. The village's name means the church of St David in the commote (a medieval Welsh secular division of land) of Efelfre. The church in question, around which a much earlier Christian settlement may have clustered beneath the Iron Age forts above, is still extant, though off the beaten track, on the no through road to the south of the village. The walk passes by it. The new expanding settlement was originally known as Commercial, taking it's name from the Commercial, an inn which developed at the settlement's crossroads, but this proved too mundane a name, and was later changed to it's present one.

The village has had a strong non conformist religious history, with, during the early 19th century, two Sunday schools from Bethel and Ffynnon chapels competing with the church's one. Llanddewi Velfrey's last school, one of many established over the years, closed in 1988. However non conformism was not without it's price; one prominent late 17th century local Quaker, Lewis David, following persecution of Quaker beliefs, found a more tolerant home in America. Prior to emigration he had, in 1681, with other Welsh Quakers, met with William Penn in London, and bought land in the colony of Pennsylvania. He later resold his land, sub divided into smaller lots, much of it to fellow Quakers with Pembrokeshire connections. By 1700 a least a third of Pennsylvania's population was Welsh.

LANDSKER

Possibly Norse in origin for frontier, the term Landsker has been used to help define the frontier which emerged with the invasions of the Normans into Pembrokeshire. With the death of the last Prince of South Wales, Rhys ap Tewdwr, in

1093, came the Norman war machine to take his lands. By the end of the year Roger of Montgomery had taken South Pembrokeshire. Under constant Welsh attack the occupation of the new lands was consolidated, if a little haphazardly; and defended by a series of forts, later to become stone castles. The frontier line stretched from Roch in the west, to Wiston, Llawhaden, Narberth, Amroth, Laugharne and Llansteffan.

The Norman pattern of the town and manorial village was established, the village often around a central green for defence, with grouped dwellings and farmhouses, a fortified manor house or castle, and a church and parsonage. Later the church acquired a high crenellated tower as lookout and last defence against encroaching Welsh. Requiring extra labour to administer the area lead to settlement of Flemings, Saxon, and English, often in the Landsker zone. The creation of *Little England beyond Wales* had begun.

North of the Landsker the landscape stayed true to the Celtic pattern, with isolated farms and villages, often divided by irregular stone wall boundaries, simple towerless churches with bellcotes, and few castles. The language remained firmly Welsh. By the 13th century the Landsker had ceased to have a military significance, yet it was to remain a cultural divide – patterns of life and landscape that can be traced today.

2. Llanddewi and Caerau Gaer Iron Age forts

Llanddewi Gaer is a massive fort, dating from the first millennium BC. Natural defences on the east and south sides are complemented by three massive banks to the north and west. Compared with the size of the banks the interior is comparatively small. The site is now somewhat overgrown. Caerau Gaer may have been an annex of Llanddewi Gaer.

3. St David's Church

Dating from at least Norman times – the church may have been built on the site of an earlier church, a circular graveyard is usually a good pointer – it has been the subject of several restorations during the 18th and 19th centuries. It is in an attractive setting, well off the beaten track, and looking out over the Marlais valley. Between 1282 and 1517 the church was known as Llanddewi Trefendeg, though no-one has been able to explain the origin of Trefendeg. From 1974 the church has been grouped with Llanddewi Velfrey. For nearly an hundred years, from 1832 to 1941, it's rectors were vice-principals or professors of St David's in Lampeter, part of the University of Wales, and the third oldest university in England and Wales after Oxford and Cambridge.

4. Llanmill

As it name suggests it once had connections with the mill industry; in this case it was, in it's heyday, a centre of the woollen industry. There were at least three fulling mills in the area, the industry thriving from the 18th century onwards. At

Lampeter Vale

one time the owner of the Llanmill business, William Humphreys, did well enough financially to lease Dyffryn mill and rebuild it on three floors, with steam power replacing water in 1898. However despite it's products winning international prizes the depression of the mid years of the 20th century spelt the industry's closure. There were successful corn mills in the area, White Mill's dated back to 1532. White House Mill, beyond Lampeter Velfrey, had water diverted into a leat to fill it's millpond. It is now a trout fishery.

5. Lampeter Velfrey
Lampeter is an Anglicisation of the Welsh Llanbedr, ie the settlement, or llan, of Peter. The church received a major restoration during the mid 19th century, with new roofs and windows. Latest restoration dates from 1998. It's bell was cast back in 1639.

WALK DIRECTIONS [-] indicates history note
1. Starting from Parc y Lan Inn in Llanddewi Velfrey [1] walk along the A40 in the Haverfordwest direction the short distance to the road access bay for houses to your left. Past houses (house names Penbryn and Efailwen), and just before the entrance to the access bay from the main road, enter a small field through a rusty gate. There is a signpost here, but it has fallen into the hedge, together with it's concrete base.

2. Keep to the right edge (there is a sunken lane, but overgrown, so keep to the field) to reach a derelict building at the bottom of the field. Keeping the building on your left (the path here can be a little muddy after rain) continue the short distance to a stream. There is a stile to the right giving access to the stream bank.

3. Cross the stream to enter a fenced area, with an attractive pond to the right. Go through the farm gate ahead, and keeping the field edge on your left continue uphill to enter more open ground, and stay ahead to reach a stile giving access to a minor road.

4. Cross the stile opposite and to the right to enter a field. Continue ahead to reach an area of woodland. An old trig point

Llanddewi Velfrey pond

is to the left, in the hedge, just before the wood is reached. Cross a stile and continue downhill, along the flanks of the old Iron Age fort – Llanddewi Gaer [2] – to reach a track.

5. Bear right and continue, passing St David's church [3] to the left, until just past a house on the left the track finally deteriorates in quality. The track itself bears left downhill, but is usually so muddy that a better route is to continue ahead to a farm gate and enter the field directly ahead.

6. Cross the field keeping to the left edge to quickly gain a track through another gate. Continue on the tack as it winds downhill, keeping to the left edge, until a small wooden gate on the left is reached.

7. Leave the track through the gate and bearing left continue downhill on a minor road until just after passing under a railway bridge bear right on a track giving access to Dyffryn farm. A large papier maché elephant has stood at the entrance to White Mill (on the right before the bridge) for a number of years, but is now not looking it's best.

8. Keep on the track to Dyffryn farm as it bears left, and keeping the buildings to your left, continue through the grounds to reach a metal gate. Go into a field and bear right. Keep to the right edge until by a waymarked post bear right across a footbridge and stile, and after going through a metal gate follow the track to a road.

9. Continue on this road to reach the minor road at Llanmill [4] – where the access road meets the Llanmill road there is in the wall to the right an old Victoria Regina letter box. Bear left and continue on the minor road, passing through Lampeter Velfrey [5], for well over a mile/two kilometres, until the entrance to White House Mill is reached.

10. Bear left and continue along a metal track through the mill grounds until where the track bends left go ahead through a gate and enter a field. Continue ahead through fields to reach the railway line

11. Cross and continue ahead across fields to reach a wooden footbridge with hand rails. Cross and enter a field. Cross this field and in the next, instead of keeping to the right edge, bear diagonally left uphill to enter another field across a stile by a gate.

12. Keeping to the right edge continue uphill to top the rise in the field. Bear left to cross the middle of the field to enter a smaller field with a wire fence on your right, and leading you ahead to Panteg.

12. On reaching the gate at the end of this field continue ahead, keeping the house on your left, and continue uphill on a track through woodland until just past farm buildings bear left onto a track leading downhill. The track shortly joins another – continue right, uphill.

13. Continue to reach a minor road and bear left, to almost immediately bear right and go ahead past houses to reach the main A40. Bear left to return to the inn.

FACILITIES
BT phone, shop, garage and café in Llanddewi Velfrey.

12. haverfordwest

5.5 miles/8.75 kilometres

Note: The path along the foreshore along the river Cleddau's banks can flood at high tide. Check the tide tables!

OS Maps: OS 1:25 000 South Pembrokeshire Outdoor Leisure 36.
Start: Bristol Trader Inn, Haverfordwest.
Access: Overlooking the river the Bristol Trader can be found on the left of Quay Street, which itself leads off to the left from Victoria Place after crossing the bridge in the centre of town. Easy access by bus and train.
Parking: Parking possible in front of the Bristol Trader, or in Quay Street.
Grade: Easy.

Bristol Trader Inn (01437 762122)
During Haverfordwest's medieval and early modern trading days the quays on the town welcomed ships from home and abroad, and with a weekly ship to Bristol the name was a true reflection of it's role. One of the town's most popular pubs a restaurant extension was added 2005.

HISTORY NOTES
1. Haverfordwest – town and castle
Haverfordwest's known history begins with the arrival of the Normans and the building of it's castle. Always an English castle throughout it's history it was reputedly established in the mid 12th century by the then Earl of Pembroke, Gilbert de Clare. It's first recorded mention was by Giraldus Cambrensis, who visited it in 1188 in company with Archbishop Baldwin. Situated on an isolated ridge, with a cliff on it's eastern side, it overlooked the river Cleddau and the lowest fording point on the river. Hence one argument for the origin of the town's name being, *haefr ford*, *haefr* being Old English for a male goat or buck.

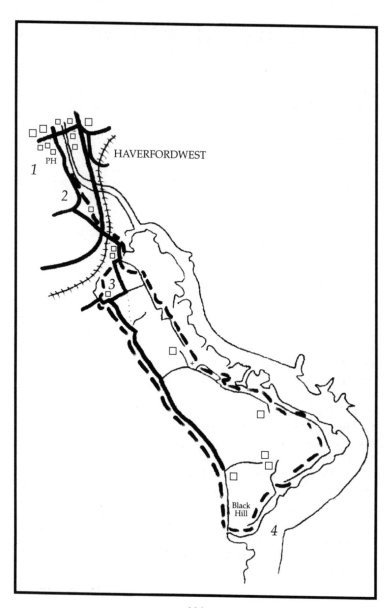

Another derives from the Viking, *Havr-Fjord*, or corn inlet. Originally built of timber and earth the castle was soon converted to stone, and withstood an attack in 1220 by Llywelyn the Great, who set fire to the existing town. In 1642, the year of the outbreak of the Civil War, the castle was in the hands of the Parliamentarians, with the town well garrisoned. However the following year saw the castle pass to the Royalists side, only to be retaken. Back in Royalist hands for four months in 1645 the castle returned to Parliament in August. In 1648 direct orders from Cromwell demanded the destruction of the castle by it's inhabitants, and at the town and county's expense, however the job seems to have been poorly executed!

The town that grew up in the shadow of the castle was defended by town walls on the high ground, though only rare traces of these remain. It's earliest extant charter was granted by Henry II (1154-1189), with incorporation by Edward, Prince of

Haverfordwest town and castle

Wales and Lord of Haverford, in 1479. Situated at the highest navigable point on the western Cleddau the town flourished as a port, with vessels of up to two hundred tons berthing at it's quays. Exports of corn, malt, wool, hides and coal went out by sea, with a weekly packet sailing to Bristol and Waterford in Ireland. A passenger vessel sailed once a month for London. Imports of iron, salt and wine arrived from France and Spain. The mayor has always also been known as the Admiral of the Port. The town was a bustling, busy market town; it's situation at the centre of the county resulting in it becoming the county town, in place of Pembroke, in 1542.

Despite gaining a reputation at one time for being the haunt of pirates the town's sea trade continued to flourish until the arrival of the first train in December 1853. The flags, banners and bunting that heralded the first locomotive spelt a farewell to Haverfordwest's sea trading days. With the arrival of the railways came the new designation of Haverford west, to distinguish it from Hereford or Hertford across the border in England. The town continued to flourish as a market town for the surrounding area, and became fashionable in the 18th and 19th centuries as the centre where the local gentry had their town houses, their balls and their banquets. Less fashionable was the building of a gaol in the inner ward of the now ruined castle in 1779. This became an asylum in 1822, and remained in operation until 1866. A more substantial three storeyed prison was also built in the outer ward, becoming in due course first the headquarters of the Pembrokeshire Constabulary, and in 1963 the Museum and Record office.

2. Haverfordwest Priory

The priory was founded in about 1200 for the Augustinian canons by the then lord of Haverford, Robert fitz Richard. The Augustinians were committed to parochial work, and thus tended to found their houses close to towns, rather than in the countryside. A major landowner in the locality gave the priory not only income, but also influence in the affairs of the growing town. As was common with the Augustinian order in general churches in the area were appropriated, and further income generated. Excavation work during the 1980s and 1990s has clarified the layout of the priory as well as revealing the priory's garden, a rare example. Laid out originally in the mid 15th century in raised narrow beds, it was interwoven with paths. There would have been gardens also in the cloister. The beds have been replanted with herbs appropriate to it's time.

3. Haroldston House

In ruins now for over some two hundred years Haroldston House was once one of the fine houses of Pembrokeshire. Probably dating from the 14th century the mansion was the birthplace, in 1527, of John Perrott, Haverfordwest's greatest benefactor. Believed to be the illegitimate son of Henry VIII he was appointed Vice-Admiral of South Wales in 1562, becoming MP for Pembrokeshire the next year. Found guilty of treason in 1592 he was sentenced to death, but died in the Tower of London before sentence could be carried out. The hall itself was adjoined by a three storey tower, called the Steward's tower, and of which part of the stairs remain.

4. River Cleddau

The mud flats here are perfect for waders and wildfowl, with a ready supply of food buried in the mud, and with fish and plants additional offerings. Resident species include herons, shelduck, and cormorants, together with Canada geese. Winter visitors include curlew, redshank and greenshank, goldeneye, plovers, teal and wigeon. Given a fine winter's evening, with the sun slowly sinking, the cry of the curlew adds a magical sound to the tapestry of wood and field, river and sky.

WALK DIRECTIONS [-] indicates history note

1. Starting from the Bristol Trader walk up the river frontage away from the town [1] to join Quay Street. Shortly bear left to enter the ruins of Haverfordwest priory [2] – there is a signpost opposite the entrance indicating *Priory*. Continue ahead

through the grounds to reach a metal gate and a footpath crossing the field ahead to the main road.

2. Cross the main road. Cross the metal barrier and continue across the railway line, to then turn right to head uphill to gain a minor road. Bear left and continue past houses following the road around to the right.

3. Where the road bends left bear right, signposted, and continue across a boardwalk to enter a field. Bear left and taking a path diagonally right through the ruins of Haroldston House [3] reach a stile in the top right hand corner of the field.

4. Bear left on the minor road to shortly turn right and continue for well over half a mile/three quarters of a kilometre to Fern Hill lodge. Continue ahead on a green lane to reach Black Hill and the river Cleddau [4] – good views open up of the houses of Little Milford to the right.

5. Bear to the left – initially the path keeps to the foreshore, but then heads inland and keeps to the right edge of a field adjacent to the river before shortly again rejoining the foreshore through

Black Hill

a metal farm gate.

6. The path alternates between foreshore and field for a mile/one and a half kilometres or so before joining a farm track after ascending steps up from the shore. Well waymarked en route. Follow the farm track as it bends right to again rejoin foreshore and bearing left cross the field ahead to reach a church to your left. Views open up ahead of Haverfordwest castle.

7. Continue ahead on the path until just after crossing a footbridge and going through a metal kissing gate bear left uphill and keeping the hedge on your left reach a stile giving access to a field. Bear diagonally right to reach another kissing gate giving access to the minor road.

8. Bear right to retrace the beginning section of the walk, bearing right into the field and then left across the railway line to reach the main road.

FACILITIES
All available in Haverfordwest.

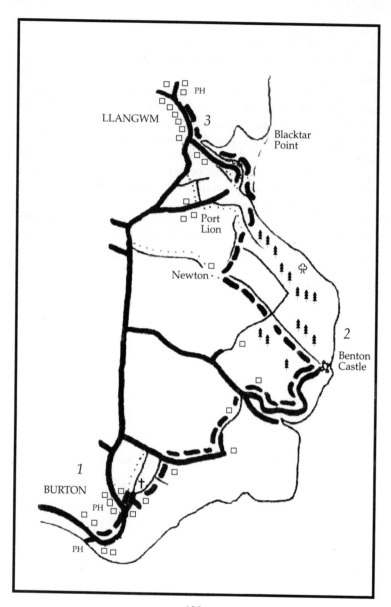

13. Burton to Llangwm

4.75 miles/7.5 kilometres

Note: At high tides the foreshore may flood at the Llangwm end of the walk – check tide tables. There is a high tide route alternative, noted in the walk directions.

OS Maps: OS 1:25 000 South Pembrokeshire Outdoor Leisure 36.
Start: Jolly Sailor in Burton Ferry.
Access: Burton is on the minor road leading off from the access road to the Cleddau Bridge on the Neyland side of the river. Bus 308 runs Mondays to Saturdays from Llangwm (Green) to Burton (and vice versa, though Burton to Llangwm will take longer as it is on a circular route). Buses across the bridge from Pembroke Dock will drop you at the turning for Burton.
Parking: By the Jolly Sailor in Burton Ferry.
Grade: Easy.

Jolly Sailor, Burton Ferry (01646 600378)

One of Pembrokeshire's most popular pubs there would have, given Burton's centuries old history as the most important ferry point on the river, been a pub of one kind or another in the village. First reference to the Jolly Sailor dates from 1809, when a local shipbuilding and shipowning family, the Deans, were at the helm, the women taking care of the pub, whilst the men built and sailed the ships. Maritime fortunes declined for the family, with the loss of vessels at sea, however the pub remained in the family's hands until into the 20th century. A series of extensions have added extra space from the 1960s onwards. An aviary at the back adds an exotic touch to the pub garden overlooking the river, and in summer months, a landing pontoon for passing craft. Good food and a good reputation.

Stable Bar, Burton (01646 600622)

Relatively recent, and converted from farm outbuildings, the

Stable Bar opened in 1976. Popular as both a pub and restaurant there is a pleasant patio garden to the back, with ample parking in front. Specialties fish and local produce. B&B available.

The Cottage, Llangwm (01437 891494)

The pub here has been in existence since 1962. Originally set up in the early 1950s as the Rock House and Cottage Club, the club served drinks to members only. Prior to this Llangwm was one amongst many of the dry villages in the county, temperance being an occurring theme in the late 19th and early 20th centuries, and leading to the closure of many existing inns. A local story tells of Maria Shrubsall, landlady of one of the earlier Llangwm pubs, the Black Horse, established in the late 19th century. She wrote to Prince Albert, son of Queen Victoria and Admiral of the Fleet, who was visiting Milford Haven with the navy, offering him a present of a black cat. The prince accepted, sending a boat up river to collect her and the cat, and giving her a fine tea aboard his ship. In return the prince's daughter and two grand daughters took tea at the Black Horse, Mrs Shrubsall reading their fortunes in the tea leaves.

HISTORY NOTES
1. Burton

Burton properly speaking is the village at the top of the hill, while Burton Ferry is the section bordering the river. Both are popular places, for leisure and for residential properties. Given it's location it has had a long association with the sea, perhaps it's heyday being during the 18th and 19th centuries when there were several shipyards. Like many strategic points along the river Burton offered a ideal point for ferrying passengers and schoolchildren by rowboat across to Pembroke Ferry on the opposite shore. Tuesdays and Fridays were special, with the fisherwomen from Llangwm further upriver being rowed across to sell their catch. The present toll bridge was opened in 1975, though not without cost – it collapsed in June 1970 due to construction errors, killing

Cleddau Bridge and Trinity House jetty

four people in the process. The timber jetty next to the Jolly Sailor (and now in need of some restoration) was built by Trinity House to provide both a landing stage and storage space. Trinity House itself, with it's name still emblazoned across it's fine gates, faces the pub, and was built in 1861 to serve as a depot for lighthouses and lightships between North Wales and Swansea, with cottages in the village providing accommodation. From 1878 to 1920 a vessel, the *Siren*, was based here, carrying lampoil as well as reliefs for crews. By 1926 the depot had transferred to Swansea. Burton's church, further up the hill in Burton village, has a 13th century nave and chancel, the transepts being added in the 14th century, and the west tower and possibly the porch dating from the 15th or 16th century. The north aisle is a Victorian addition.

2. Benton Castle

Well camaflauged among the trees lining the banks of the Daugleddau Benton castle's whitewashed prominence can be discerned rising above the treetops. Now privately owned it has been restored and rebuilt since the 1930s, up until then it had

Daugleddau river and Preseli hills

been unoccupied and in ruins since reduction during the Civil War in the mid 17th century. Using stone fallen from the walls, and oak timbers from Milford Haven shipyards, Ernest Pegge turned it into what is now a fine private residence, adding his own mask in concrete above the entrance as a final flourish. One of the original Norman castles defending territory gained during the occupation of South Wales it dates from the 13th century, and is believed to have been built by Bishop Beck of St David's. No access.

3. Llangwm

For centuries Pembrokeshire villages bordering the coast and the major rivers relied on the sea for communication, developing in the process their own unique character. Llangwm has always had a reputation for it's independence and occasional dislike of strangers; though with modern roads and lifestyle it is now a welcoming place. Like Burton Llangwm had it's own ferry, linking it with Landshipping across the water;

sometimes to Pembroke Dock down river. There has been a long association with fishing, whether from small tarred boats for herring or bass, or for harvesting of the local oysters and cockles. Llangwm women travelled far to sell their catches, either on foot or with their donkeys and carts, leaving them by the local ferries when they crossed the river – though they often rowed themselves across the river, ignoring the ferries altogether. By the beginning of the 20th century fishing had begun to decline, with more attractive wages on offer in the local towns of Neyland and Pembroke Dock. Black Tar, with it's modern concrete slipway, and from where the fishing boats used to set sail, is still busy, nowadays with both leisure and the occasional more modern fishing boat, the name a reminder of the protective tarring applied to the old craft. For two weeks during Llangwm's summer festival held at the beginning of July there is a scarecrow competition to see who can come up with the best; all variety of shapes and forms appear in front gardens and along the roads and river banks – one eighteen foot Shrek proved to be very popular. Village events, the local carnival, and a longboat regatta are all part of the mix.

WALK DIRECTIONS [-] indicates history note

1. Starting from the car parking area by the Jolly Sailor in Burton Ferry [1] walk uphill to reach Burton village. By the Stable Bar take the tuning right into Church Road and continue downhill, keeping ahead to reach Burton church.

2. Once at the church bear right in front of the building, and just before a farm gate ascend steps to reach a path passing alongside the church grounds, and shortly gain a farm track. Keep ahead keeping to the left edge, and enter a field containing an electric pylon. Continue ahead along the left side to gain a metal kissing gate.

3. Bear right and continue, passing Beggars Reach Country hotel on the right, until the road becomes a farm track. Continue on the well defined track to reach a tarmac road. Cross, and passing

Llangwm Ferry

between two stone gate posts continue around to the right, and stay on the metal track to reach Benton castle [2].

4. The path from Benton castle becomes a well defined path. Continue ahead through woodland to reach a T junction with another well defined track bordering open fields ahead. Turn right and then almost immediately left to cross a stile into fields. Continue along the right edge of two fields – great views over the river.

5. Where the track bends slightly left, and then straightens, leading towards Newton ahead, leave the track, and crossing a stile enter a wooded green lane on the right. Continue ahead, downhill, crossing a forestry track en route, to reach the foreshore. Bear left along the foreshore.

Note: If there is a high tide the foreshore will be flooded; if so bear left along the forestry track to emerge at a minor road. Bear left uphill and after a short distance bear right at a footpath sign, and cross a stile to enter a field. Continue ahead to reach a stile and fourway signpost. Continue ahead across the field to reach a stile giving access to the road leading right into Llangwm [3] and the finishing point.

6. If taking the foreshore route once at the point where a minor road meets the bay choice to continue along the foreshore, or ascend on a path to the left of a fence leading down to the bay, to shortly cross a stile and metal bars at a parking bay. Cross into the field ahead and continue ahead to reach a minor road.

7. Whichever route taken bear right at the T junction leading away from Llangwm Ferry to reach the finishing point at the Green in the centre of the village – the Cottage is a little further uphill on the right.

FACILITIES
Public toilets, and telephone at Burton Ferry. All facilities available in Llangwm. Both good for boating enthusiasts

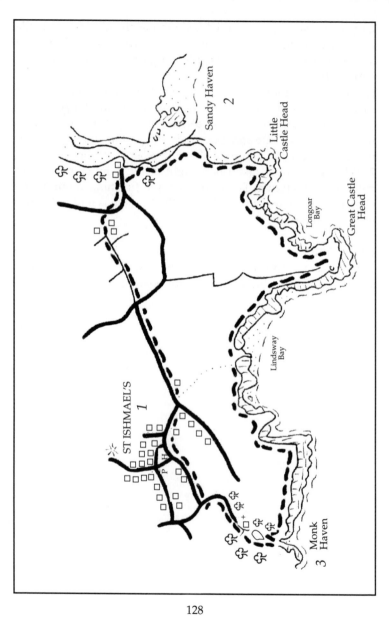

Sandy Haven

2

Little Castle Head

Great Castle Head

Longoar Bay

Lindsway Bay

ST ISHMAEL'S

1

Monk Haven

3

14. st ishmael's and sandy haven

5.25 miles / 8.5 kilometres

OS Maps: OS 1:25 000 South Pembrokeshire Outdoor Leisure 36.
Start: The Brook Inn, St Ishmael's.
Access: St Ishmael's is on a minor road leading off south from the B4327 Haverfordwest to Dale road, and is closer to Dale. No. 315/400 coastal service the Puffin Shuttle operates throughout the year. Bus stop outside the pub.
Parking: Parking in St Ishmael's or by St Ishmael's church on the road leading down to Monk Haven.
Grade: Moderate.

The Brook Inn
(01646 636277)

An attractive inn with it's own garden area the Brook Inn has been serving pints since it's conversion from a private house to a pub in 1867. At one time, during the mid 20th century, the garden was also home to a pigsty, where a succession of pigs, all named Dennis, were housed. Fed on beer slops they must have led happy, if perhaps unsteady, lives.

HISTORY NOTES

1. St Ishmael's

A village of some 480 people St Ishmael's is set down in a dip, out of the way of the wind. A popular place, with a few holiday homes, the village takes it's name from St Ishmael, an nephew of St Teilo and a disciple of St David. He is believed to have created a prayer house near Great Castle Head, and the finding of a cliff cemetery at Longoar Bay, by Great Castle Head gives credence to this. Following a cliff fall in 2001 bones were revealed in the cliff face, however investigation and excavation had to wait until 2004 when Extreme Archaeology, a TV company specializing in excavating normally inaccessible sites, undertook a detailed study by means of rigging up a platform on the cliff face to work from. Seven graves of several were uncovered, five in the cliff face, two on the cliff top – one grave had on the underside of the slab covering it a carved cross, possibly so marked as to be the first thing seen on Judgment Day. The stone is now in the National Museum, the site itself filled in. Bones from the site were carbon dated to 734 AD, though the site would have been in use for burials over a much longer period. St Ishmael's attractive church, set in the secluded valley leading down to Monk Haven, is medieval in origin, and has been dated back to 940 AD, but may be earlier. It's bell cote may have replaced an earlier tower. The porch is fronted by a stream, access across a footbridge to the cemetery. One notable medieval resident was 12th century St Caradoc of Llancarvon, who after being driven away by the Norse from his island retreat was given residence at the monastery of St Ishmael's by the Bishop of St David's. No trace of any monastery remains, however St Caradoc may well have reconstructed any existing church building. His remains are housed in St David's cathedral, and there is a shrine there to him. With the coming of the Normans to Pembrokeshire a motte castle was built to the north of the village, though of it now only the mound remains.

Sandy Haven

2. Sandy Haven bay

Some 1.25 miles/2 kilometres wide the bay framed by South Hook Point and Great Castle Head encloses Sandy Haven's beach, the lesser bays either side of Little Castle Head, and Longoar Bay by Great Castle Head. Sandy Haven pill runs inshore for well over a mile/2 kilometres making crossing to Sandy Haven on foot only possible at low tides over the stepping stones. Once the tide is in it is a long walk back inland along the roads to regain the crossing point! The area between here, Dale, and across the water to Angle, provide the best sea fishing area in the haven. South Hook Point was the site of the old Esso oil refinery, Milford Haven's first. Opened in 1960 it was closed in 1983. The site is now being utilised by South Hook LNG (Liquefied Natural Gas), one of two LNG sites in the haven, the other being Dragon LNG further up river by Neyland. The circular fort in the bay is much older; Stack Rock formed part of the defensive forts built during the mid 19th

131

century fears of a French invasion. An even earlier presence is indicated by Iron Age forts at both Little and Great Castle Heads, the latter's dating back to circa 300 BC.

3. Monk Haven

The small cove of Monk Haven was a favourite landing place during the Age of the Saints and the Middle Ages, with travellers and pilgrims preferring to use the old Neolithic and Bronze Age trackway from Monk Haven as a safe route to St David's, thus avoiding the hazards and dark moods of the sea. The sandstone wall across the head of the beach was built in the 18th century as an estate boundary. The ruined two storey watch tower on the approach to Monk Haven, at the end of an estate wall, is a folly dating to circa 1860, and is known as the Malakov after the architect, who served during the Crimean War – *Malakhov* was a fortified hill overlooking Sevastopol. Clearly visible around the coast here are the layers of Old Red Sandstone which underlie most of the Milford Haven area.

WALK DIRECTIONS [-] indicates history note

1. Starting from the Brook Inn in St Ishmael's [1] walk uphill on the road leading out of the village, passing the school on the way – this is Trewarren road. Continue past the sports ground to reach a T junction.

2. Continue ahead across fields, keeping to the left hand side initially, and then gaining a short path cross into a second field and keeping to the right edge continue to reach Sandy Haven farm.

3. Bear right at the minor road and continue until where the road bends around sharp right bear left onto the road leading down to Sandy Haven. There is a lime kiln and a cattle weighing machine on the right here.

4. A short distance on the right the route continues on the Coast Path, up steps to a gate, however it is worthwhile to continue the short distance to Sandy Haven [2] before rejoining the route.

5. Once back on the route the path leads on to Little and Great

Castle Heads, passing the navigation marker of Little Castle Head Beacon. On from Great Castle Head the path passes St Ishmael's beach at Lindsway Bay – steep steps down – to finally reach Monk Haven [3]. The MoD bunkers passed en route were manned in both World Wars.

6. From Monk Haven take the path leading inland, passing the church on your right, and continue on the minor road uphill to bear right onto the minor road leading back down to St Ishmael's and the starting point.

FACILITIES

Post office/shop, public telephone. Toilets by the sports ground – sometimes locked. Popular garden centre to the north of the village.

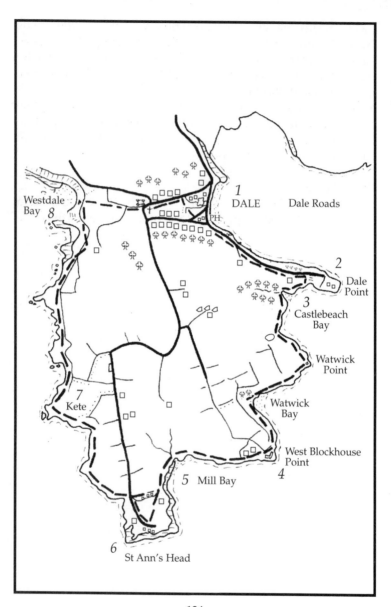

Westdale Bay *8*

1 DALE

Dale Roads

PH

2 Dale Point

3 Castlebeach Bay

Watwick Point

Watwick Bay

West Blockhouse Point

4

7 Kete

5 Mill Bay

6 St Ann's Head

15. Dale

7 miles/11 kilometres

OS Maps: OS 1:25 000 South Pembrokeshire Outdoor Leisure 36.
Start: The Griffin Inn in Dale.
Access: Dale is 11 miles from Haverfordwest on the B4327, and is within easy reach of Broad Haven and Little Haven, and St Brides Haven and Marloes. Bus 315/400 operates from Haverfordwest to Dale. (Puffin shuttle).
Parking: Dale car park – on the right as you enter Dale.
Grade: Moderate – a little road walking, but mostly coastal path.

The Griffin Inn (01646 636227)

There have been a number of pubs in Dale in it's history, however the Griffin is the sole survivor. Originally the Three Horseshoes an incoming landlord changed it to the Griffin in 1824, though why is not known. The Griffin is one of the most popular inns on the coast, with the harbour wall outside a popular spot for sitting and watching the activity in the bay during the warmer months. Real fire in season, beer garden.

HISTORY NOTES

1. Dale

Dale's written history begins in 1293 when a Robert de Vale was granted a charter to hold a weekly market and an annual fair. The present castle, a private residence, probably occupies the original castle's site. The medieval church, with it's 15th century tower, is dedicated to St James, and was substantially restored in the 1890s. By Tudor times Dale was a place of some importance, certainly so far as the Milford Haven is concerned Dale and Angle, on the opposite shore, were the largest villages, with Dale vying with Fishguard for size. Three eight to nine ton trading ships were owned, and Dale became known in Liverpool and Bristol for it's fine ale. Fortunes seem to have declined by the 1800s however, with the village fallen into ruins, but by the 1850s two ships totalling forty three tons had been built, and fishing, shipbuilding and general trading were again to the fore. The four prominent buildings overlooking the bay and which line what was once Dale's quay all date from the 17th/18th centuries. Whilst Dale is noted as the sunniest place in Wales, the Dale peninsula makes up for it by being one of the windiest in Britain! Dale's forté is now water sports, though there is still good ale to be had. Often used as an overnight anchorage by ocean going yachts, Dale Roads played host to many of the finest sailing ships in the world during the Tall Ships race in 1991.

2. Dale Point

There was an Iron Age fort here by 300 BC – the single bank and ditch are clearly visible, running out across the headland, with the former entrance in the middle of the bank. Dale Fort was built as part of Milford Haven's 19th century defensive system between 1852 and 1856, the road leading to it from Dale being the old military access road. The fort was taken over in 1947 by

Dale and the Griffin Inn

the Field Studies Council who run courses mainly in marine biology, though geology, geography, archaeology and painting also find a place. Good views from the headland over Dale Roads.

3. Castlebeach Bay

Castlebeach is a pleasant wooded bay with a sandy beach. There is an old lime kiln at the head of the beach where limestone quarried at West Williamston, near Lawrenny, or on Caldey island, would have been burnt to provide lime for local farms as fertilizer or mortar. Now overgrown there are the ruins of the lime burner's cottage in the wood. Lime burning had largely died out by the beginning of the 20th century, the last recorded use of kilns in the Dale area was at Pickleridge in the 1920s.

4. West Blockhouse Point

West Blockhouse Point derives it's name from the Victorian fort built here as part of Milford Haven's fortifications. The first attempt to fortify the Haven was undertaken by Henry VIII, with blockhouses on both northern and southern sides of the Haven entrance, but of these only that at Angle survives. Further fortifications had to wait until the mid 19th century when fears of French invasion led to a more thorough system. West Blockhouse was matched by another fort, now demolished, on the opposite shore, by Rat island at East Angle; Dale Fort was matched by the island fort on Thorn island; the circular island fort on Stack Rock by Popton Fort, by Angle Bay; and so on down the Haven, until the Defensible Barracks, holding the main defence force of five hundred men, was reached at the new Royal Naval Dockyard at Pembroke Dock. The whole system, complete by 1875, was overseen by General Gordon of Khartoum fame. Obsolete as soon as built, and without a shot having been fired, these forts became known as Palmerston's Follies – after Palmerston, at various times Prime Minister and Foreign Secretary during mid century. The fort here was built by 1857 for eighty men, and was at last utilized during both World Wars, for anti-aircraft defence. By 1950 the fort was abandoned, and is now the property of the Landmark Trust, in use for holiday letting.

The three navigation towers, together with that on Watwick Point, were built in 1970. By holding the central tower here in transit with that on Watwick Point, shipping is led into the deep water channel. There is a similar system of buildings and towers on Great Castle Head for the next deep channel section. The pilot or master of the vessel aligns the lights, or the white or black lines. At night the lights have a possible range of nineteen miles/thirty kilometres, the red lights on the two outer towers here indicating the channel entrance. Watwick Point tower currently ranks as one of the tallest lighthouses in the world. They are under the jurisdiction of the Milford Haven Port Authority.

5. Mill Bay

Mill Bay, just before sunset on Sunday 7 August 1485, was the unlikely host to the beginnings of one of the great adventures of British history, when Henry Tudor came ashore from Brittany, with his fleet of fifty thousand ships and four thousand men landing at nearby Dale, to begin his lightning march to Stafford, Bosworth Field, and the English crown. Born in nearby Pembroke castle in 1459, Henry had been left sole heir to the Lancastrian throne following the Wars of the Roses, and had had to seek refuge in France. Recalled in 1485 Henry landed on home territory to meet enthusiastic support, many hailing him as the new King Arthur. By 22 August Richard III was dead, the Tudor age inaugurated, and Henry VII on the throne.

The wreck here is that of a boom defence vessel which broke away from the tug towing it for scrap in 1964. One earlier disaster from the days of sail – the Mill Bay disaster – occurred in September 1866. The leader of a group of six or seven sailing ships running before a gale in poor visibility went aground – the others followed suit with disastrous loss of life.

6. St Ann's Head

There was once a small chapel here, dedicated to St Ann, mother of Mary and patron saint of Brittany, and quite possibly established by Henry VII in thanks for his victory at Bosworth Field. There was a twenty foot/six metres high tower light attached to the chapel, a great boon to ships entering the Haven. However the chapel was demolished during the Reformation, though the tower light was rebuilt. A second lighthouse was built in 1714, which comprised two towers lit by coal. The front tower was rebuilt further inland in 1841, and was modernised in 1958 when it was put onto electricity. The rear light became the coastguard station in 1910. The small tower house contains the foghorn. The old coastguard and Trinity House cottages and the coastguard station are now in private ownership. The walled garden and stone quay nearby date from 1800, the latter built for transporting materials for the lighthouse. A new thin steel towered lighthouse was built out at sea, just off the Head, in 1966, to mark the entrance to the deep water channel – the Mid Channel Rocks Lighthouse.

The area between St Ann's Head, across to the Angle peninsula and flat topped Linney Head, is known locally as the Heads. At one time the Bristol Channel was mostly land, and the river then flowing through the Haven would have continued across the plain to join the Severn almost halfway between St Ann's Head and Lands End in Cornwall, but with the end of the Ice Age the meltwater flooded the Haven, creating a ria, or drowned river valley, much along present lines. The mouth of the Haven is one and a quarter miles/two kilometres wide, and eighteen miles/thirty kilometres long, navigable as far as Haverfordwest and Canaston Bridge. The decision to create a major oil port was taken in the late 1950s, Esso the first refinery to open in 1960. Some veritable giants of tankers are now common fare; however there are some that come to grief. In October 1978 the Greek tanker *Christos Bitas* went aground on the Hats and Barrels reef, near Grassholm island, spilling thirty five thousand tons of oil. As a result of this incident the Centre for Oiled Birds was established at West

Williamston, near Carew. The Centre was well occupied in February 1996 when the *Sea Empress* went aground on the shoals and rocks below St Ann's Head, spilling seventy thousand tons of light crude oil in the six days it took to tow her off the rocks.

7. Bird islands and HMS Harrier

Great views from here of the islands of Skokholm, Grassholm and Skomer – life on this side of the peninsula is much quieter than the activity and bustle of the Haven. Ronald Lockley made Skokholm his island home from 1927 to 1939, establishing Britain's first bird observatory there in 1933. His two books, *Dream Island* and *Island Days*, describe his life, where he *resolved to imitate* [Thoreau's] *austere mode of living when I at last came to dwell on my dream island.* Together with Skomer and Grassholm these islands represent some of the finest seabird colonies in Europe, with shearwaters, gannets, razorbills, guillemots, choughs and the splendid puffins. They can be reached from Martin's Haven, near Marloes. During the medieval period the islands provided it's owners with a good steady income derived from the farming of rabbits. In the ownership of Dale castle estate since 1646 Skokholm was bought, following the death of the last owner in 2005, by the Wildlife Trust of South and West Wales in 2006.

Kete was the site of HMS Harrier, a Royal Navy radar and meteorological school, which closed in 1960. The land was bought by the National Trust in 1967, buildings cleared, and the area returned to agricultural use. The former married quarters in Dale are now private residences. In it's heyday Kete was used to train radar technicians and fighter direction officers, whose task it was to detect enemy aircraft prior to their attack on friendly shipping, and to direct fighter planes to deal with them. Mock battles were fought over the local seaways out to the Smalls lighthouse. In it's early days there were no aircraft that could be spared for training purposes so former Walls ice cream tricycles became a useful weapon of war – one set of trikes became an enemy bomber, it's course steered by compass, whilst the others, once the enemy trikes had been spotted by the radar operator, were sent to attack them. They were later replaced by the real planes and electronic simulators. The base provided for some eight hundred people. There is a memorial plaque, with a photograph of the site, in Kete car park.

8. Westdale Bay

Unlike Dale Westdale Bay has a sandy beach, but beware of the strong undertow on the ebb tide if you are planning to swim. Overlooking the bay on the south side is the Iron Age fort on Great Castle Head, dating from circa 100 BC. It has massive banks and ditches, and is particularly impressive on the approach from Kete. The entrance makes good use of the rock faulting. To the north, again overlooking the bay, are the remains of the old Dale airfield, which was to transfer to Brawdy, near Newgale. The route from Westdale back to Dale follows the course of an old river valley, and, but for the fall in sea level, Dale peninsula would have remained an island.

WALK DIRECTIONS [-] indicates history note

1. Starting from Dale [1] walk past the Griffin Inn and Dale Yacht Club and follow the tarmac road to Dale Fort Field Centre.
2. Just before the Field Centre views open up, left, over Dale Roads. To the right is access to the coastal path and the headland overlooking Dale Point [2].
3. Follow the Coast Path from Dale Point on to Castlebeach Bay [3], and continue on past the navigation beacon on Watwick Point to the sandy beach of Watwick Bay – a popular bay in summer. Access to the beach down a narrow footpath.
4. Continue to West Blockhouse Point [4], and Mill Bay's small rocky inlet [5], to arrive at St Ann's Head, [6] guarding the entrance to the Milford Haven.
5. The tarmac road leads two miles/three kilometres back to Dale – continue however the two and a half miles/four kilometres on the Coast Path around to Kete [7] and Westdale Bay [8].

6. From Westdale Bay – easy access to the beach down convenient steps – cross the stone stile to the right of the Coast Path, and continue inland across the centre of the field to join the farm track leading to Hayguard Hay farm.

7. Continue ahead on the farm track to shortly join the road leading back into Dale and the starting point. Choice of road, or footpath across the fields by Dale car park.

FACILITIES

Free parking in the National Trust car park at Kete – there is no official car parking at St Ann's Head. Limited parking is also possible in the parking bay above Westdale Bay – follow the road behind Dale castle. All facilities are available in Dale. A very popular centre for water sports.

16. MARLOES

7 miles / 11 kilometres

OS Maps: OS 1:25 000 South Pembrokeshire Outdoor Leisure 36.
Start: The Lobster Pot Inn in Marloes.
Access: Marloes is one mile/0.75 kilometres west of the B4327 Haverfordwest to Dale road. Bus 315/400 Haverfordwest to Marloes and Dale. (Puffin shuttle).
Parking: Parking possible by the Lobster Pot Inn, or else there is a small parking bay just by the footpath turning to Musselwick. National Trust car parks also at Marloes Sands and the Deer Park.
Grade: Moderate.

Lobster Pot Inn (01646 636233)
There were a number of pubs in Marloes during the course of the 19th century, however the last of them were reputably closed in the 1880s by the local landowner Lord Kensington, a keen advocate of the temperance movement. The purpose built Lobster Pot opened it's doors in November 1962, and has proved a popular venue over the years. Beer garden to rear.

HISTORY NOTES
1. Marloes
Marloes has the distinction of being the most westerly village in Wales – from here the road leads only to the Deer Park. It derives it's name from the welsh, moel rhos, ie *bare moor.* Yet despite it's Welsh linguistic heritage it

Marloes' clock tower

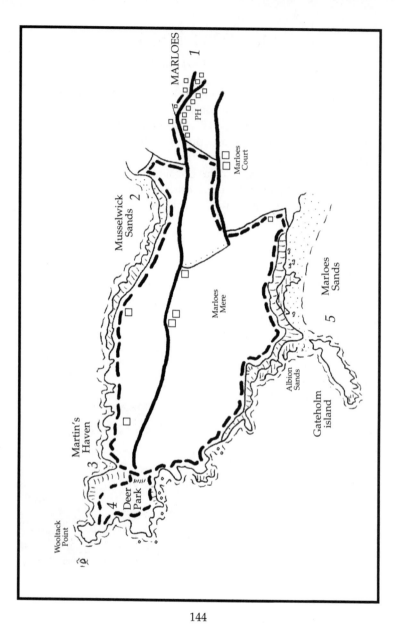

MARLOES 1

PH

Marloes Court

Musselwick Sands 2

Marloes Mere

Marloes Sands

3

5

Martin's Haven

3

4 Deer Park

Albion Sands

Gateholm island

Wooltack Point

shows similarity in layout with English villages, and with other similar villages in south Pembrokeshire. The local church, St Peters, was restored in the 1870s. One noticeable architectural feature is the clock tower, built in 1904 by Lady Kensington, widow of William, the 4th Lord Kensington, who died in 1896. A plaque on the tower notes it's erection by members of the Pembrokeshire Liberal Association. It is said to have been built as a reminder of Lord Kensington's punctuality. As Barons of Kensington the Edwardes family noted their Pembrokeshire interests on the London map; Marloes Road vies with Edwardes Square, Pembroke Road with Nevern Place. Marloes mere, drained and now a wetland, at one time provided London's Harley Street medical practitioners with medicinal leeches.

2. Musselwick

Musselwick Sands, tucked away out of reach of the prevailing south westerlies, has a fine sandy beach. Good swimming, and fewer crowds than at the better known Marloes Sands. Beware of being cut off by an incoming tide, these are not the cliffs to climb in a hurry! At the beginning of the Mesolithic era Musselwick would have been well inland, but with the demise of the great northern ice fields the peats, woods and marshes favoured by Mesolithic hunters vanished slowly under the sea – the soft red sandstones fell victim to the waves, while the hard volcanic rocks of the Deer Park and St David's Head stood resistant, and remain to frame St Brides Bay. From Musselwick north to nearby Nab Head the soft reds and purples mingle with the harder black shales; at Musselwick itself the uniform black of the rocky path down to the beach confirms the change to harder rock. Excavations at Nab Head have revealed the site of a Mesolithic/Neolithic flint chipping factory. Axe and arrow heads, simple tools including scraping tools for cleaning skins, as well as, unusually for a site of this type, more than six hundred perforated stone beads, have been found. There are displays in Tenby museum.

3. Martin's Haven
From Martin's Haven, Marloes' harbour, boats leave for the islands of Skomer and Skokholm, home to one of the great bird shows of Britain. Don't miss it! At one time Marloes fishermen sailed out to camp on Grassholm's gannet island in search of lobster and crayfish. Sea birds provided good bait; and eating. Nowadays the gannets are left strictly to themselves. During the construction of the public toilets in the 1980s a stone cross, dated to between AD 600 to 900 was unearthed, and is now housed in the wall flanking the path down to the beach.

4. The Deer Park
Despite it's name the Deer Park has never held deer; a walled enclosure, still extant, was built alongside the valley running from Martin's Haven across the park in the 18th century to house them, but it was never put to purpose. The high bank and ditch above the valley inside the park formed a defensive feature of a former Iron Age settlement. The bracken and gorse are kept to manageable lengths by Welsh mountain ponies – areas of close cropped grassland are much favoured the local choughs, a common sighting with their distinctive red legs and beaks a fine contrast to their black crow's sheen. The beaches around the Deer Park provide good pupping grounds for the local seals during autumn. Well worth walking up to Wooltack Point for the excellent views over Skomer island and St Brides Bay. Jack Sound, between the point and Midland Isle, has a fearsome reputation, it's tide races leading to disaster for many ships – nearby Albion Sands takes it's name from the

Deer Park seals

wreck of the packet *Albion,* run ashore after she was holed on a rock in the sound in 1837; two iron shafts of her remain, pointing to heaven.

5. Marloes Sands and Gateholm Island

One of the finest and most picturesque beaches in Wales the sands are a fine place to spent an afternoon's sunbathing during the summer months, and provide good swimming. One notable geological feature of the sands is the Three Chimneys – beds of Silurian sandstone and mudstone upended to stand vertically, the three slabs easily identifiable. The Old Red Sandstone rock of Gateholm island (from the Norse *goat island*) is home to the ruined settlement of the early mediaeval period – finds of Roman pottery and coins from the 3rd or 4th century date at least some of the settlement to the later Roman period. Though mostly well hidden under the vegetation there are the footings of at least a hundred buildings built either side of a central trackway, perhaps established when Gateholm may have been a

Marloes Sands

promontory of the Marloes peninsula. Findings of French ceramics from the 11th to 13th century suggest later use. The purpose of the site is not known, perhaps a monastic settlement or a secular site. Difficult of access.

WALK DIRECTIONS [-] indicates history note

1. Starting from the Lobster Pot Inn in Marloes [1] walk up the minor road leading to the Deer Park. After a short distance, by a rough parking bay, bear right and continue to reach both the Coast Path and the path leading down to Musselwick Sands [2].

2. Bear left to join the Coast Path and continue on to Martin's Haven [3]. The Coast Path continues around the Deer Park [4], though there is a short cut across the neck of the park if preferred. Continue on to Marloes Sands [5], passing Gateholm island en route – there is a rough track leading down to the sands on the Marloes side of the Coast Path, on the peninsula overlooking the island.

3. Once at Marloes Sands take the path leading up from the beach to reach a minor road. Bear right and continue the short distance to reach Marloes Court on the right. Bear left on a footpath and cross fields to reach the minor road leading back to Marloes. Bear right to regain the starting point.

FACILITIES

Post office and shop in Marloes. Public toilets and telephone opposite the Lobster Pot Inn and public toilets also at Martin's Haven. There is a hide overlooking Marloes mere – easily reached on the path leading past the youth hostel at Marloes Sands.

17. Little Haven

3.25 miles/5 kilometres

OS Maps: OS 1:25 000 South Pembrokeshire Outdoor Leisure 36.
Start: Little Haven.
Access: Little Haven is on the coast 1 mile/1.5 kilometres to the south of Broad Haven, which is reached on the B4341 from Haverfordwest.
Parking: Car park in Little Haven – seasonal charge. Free parking in the parking bay above Musselwick and Goultrop Roads (on the coastal road leading south out of Little Haven). Coastal bus service 400 calls at Little Haven, service 311 from Haverfordwest calls at Little Haven's sister village Broad Haven.
Grade: Easy.

The Castle (01437 781445) www.castlelittlehaven.co.uk
Once the British Hotel it was renamed the Castle during the mid 19th century. The Castle has had the reputation as being one of the most haunted pubs in Britain, with restless footsteps and objects being mysteriously moved. It has been recently attractively refurbished, and is now a mixture of traditional and modern open plan. Terrace area in front of the building, adjacent to Little Haven's green, and with great views overlooking beach and bay. Specialties include fish, local meat, lobster and crab. Separate dining area. Two guest bedrooms, and cottage available.

St Bride's Inn (01437 781266)
Once the New Inn the rather more imposing sounding St Bride's Inn is an attractive building, with a sheltered and sunny garden area just across the road. Inside there is a

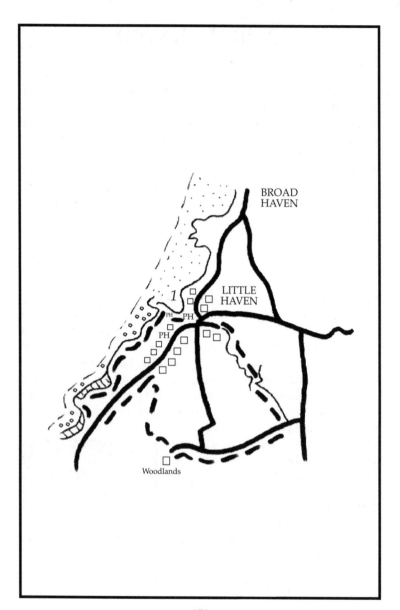

BROAD
HAVEN

LITTLE
HAVEN

1

PH PH

PH

Woodlands

stone bar with pews for seating, the bar connecting with the dining area. The well in the bar grotto may date back to Roman times. Open fire in season. Accommodation available.

The Swan Inn (01437 781880)
Recently refurbished and re-opened the Swan has long been one of Pembrokeshire's most popular pubs, with the sea wall outside the inn providing a favourite perch for those hot summer evenings. The inn is probably named after an Alexander Swann, who ran a pub in the village from the late 18th to early 19th centuries.

HISTORY NOTES
1. Little Haven
Little Haven, set deep in a valley facing out into St Brides Bay, is very much a Cornish style village. It's development was due to the coal that was mined from small pits in the immediate neighbourhood, including the steep cliffs that run on to Broad Haven, and the fact that it's beach afforded one of the best and safest loading beaches along this stretch of coast. With the demise of the coal trade the trading smacks that once beached directly onto the shore for loading were replaced by pleasure craft and rented fishing boats, and the village has developed as one of the most popular areas in Pembrokeshire. However even in recent years it has been not entirely unknown for someone to wander down to the cliffs with a bucket and hack away for a night's coal, though rewards have become sparse! At low tide Little Haven's sandy beach links with Broad Haven's, providing one of the county's most popular strolls.

The cliffs here have been much folded giving rise to a series of synclines and anticlines; there is a small cave carved out by the sea just as the cliffs turn to the Settlands from Little Haven, and known locally as the Fox Hole. Another popular walk is the short stroll out to the Point, with it's fine panorama. Little Haven's lifeboat is now stationed in the village, but at one time

Little Haven and the Swan Inn

the slipway was at Goultrop, situated below the coast path that runs out towards Borough Head to the left of the haven, and the equipment for the station was housed in Point Cottage, the building in front of the steps leading up to the cliff top from the Point. The boat itself was a sailing lifeboat, equipped with twelve oars, and operated for some forty years until difficulties in obtaining a crew forced it's closure in 1921.

WALK DIRECTIONS [-] indicates history note
1. Starting from Little Haven **[1]** walk past the Swan Inn towards the Point. Good views from here over St Brides Bay. Proceed up the steps to the left of the Point to gain the Coast Path. Continue to reach a small parking area above Musselwick.
2. Turn left and continue downhill on the road into Little Haven to turn sharp right opposite Glen Court, and by Rookery Nook. Just past the play area, and before houses, bear left on a signposted footpath, and crossing a footbridge bear right and

continue through woodland.

3. At Woodvale and Woodlands bear left on the minor road and continue to reach a junction. Continue straight on, to bear left through a metal kissing gate at a signpost to enter a field. Follow the right edge, and then continuing down along a wooded dip in the field bear right to cross the stream and gain a stile.

4. Cross the stile and bearing left continue ahead across the field to reach a stone stile giving access to Wesley Road. Continue ahead to regain the starting point.

FACILITIES

Public toilets in Little Haven. Also Bistro, Post Office/shop and public phone box.

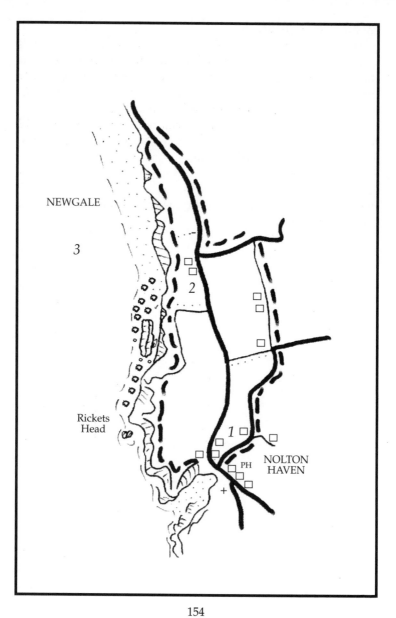

NEWGALE

3

2

Rickets
Head

1

PH

NOLTON
HAVEN

18 nolton haven

3.6 miles/5.75 kilometres

OS Maps: OS 1:25 000 South Pembrokeshire Outdoor Leisure 36.
Start: The Mariners' Inn.
Access: Nolton Haven is on the coast road between Newgale and Broad Haven.
Parking: Free car park to rear of the Mariners' Inn in Nolton Haven. Coastal bus service 400 calls at Nolton Haven.
Grade: Moderate – steep sections at Rickets Head and by Trefrane colliery ruins.

The Mariners' Inn (01437 710469)
The inn dates from 1794, when it was originally a smugglers' inn. Now privately owned and managed it has an attractive interior with a seafaring theme, including a large glass case housing Albert the albatross. Outside garden area overlooking the bay. En suite accommodation available.

HISTORY NOTES
1. Nolton Haven
The present appearance of this attractive sandy cove belies it's bustling industrial heritage. Nolton, and the cliffs along to Newgale, form part of the Pembrokeshire coalfield, it's rich anthracite seams mined especially during the 18th and 19th centuries. The mined coal was loaded onto trolleys, which were in turn pulled, first by horse, and then by traction engine, to Nolton Haven for loading onto waiting ships – the route of the tramway can still be traced. The counting house, where account was taken of the number of wagon loads of coal for export, still stands to the side of the old tramway, on the corner almost opposite the entrance to the caravan site, on what is now the minor road leading down to the haven. Long disappeared the quay, where the coal was loaded, was built on the northern side of the beach in 1769. The embankment, where coal was stored

prior to shipment, is to the seaward side of the coast road.

2. Trefrane Colliery ruins

Mining in one form or another can be traced back to 1439, however the 18th and 19th centuries saw the height of it's industrial exploitation. At one time there were six main collieries dotted between Nolton and Newgale – the ruined chimney stack here belonged to Trefrane Cliff Colliery, the chimney's purpose to create an updraft of air for ventilation. In operation from circa 1850 to 1905 its galleries ran out under the sea. Little remains except for the stack, the foundations of the engine house and other colliery buildings, and heaps of colliery waste. There were plans to reopen it in 1915, with a railway line to Milford Haven for export, however nothing was done to implement it. Nowadays it is home to the resident bird population, including that rare member of the crow family the chough, with it's distinctive red beak and legs contrasting smartly with it's black plumage.

Nolton Haven

3. St Brides Bay

Great views all along this stretch of coast over St Brides Bay and the islands of Skomer and Ramsey. On clear days good views of Grassholm island, to the right of Skomer, and ten miles/sixteen kilometres offshore. Home to some 35,000 pairs of gannets it is one of the largest gannet colonies in the world, and the only gannet colony in Wales. Newgale, with it's two mile stretch of sand, is Pembrokeshire's longest beach and one of the county's most popular all year round attractions, particularly in winter with it's surf flying in off the sea. It is one of Pembrokeshire's storm beaches, it's ridge of pebbles thrown up by winter storms. At very low tides it is possible to pick out the remains of the blackened tree stumps of the forest which once covered St Brides Bay before the sea came in to claim overlordship. The bay provides haven for tankers waiting entrance to Milford Haven's energy terminals.

WALK DIRECTIONS [-] indicates history note

1. Starting from the Mariners' Inn join the coast path ascending to the right of Nolton Haven [1], and continue on to Rickets Head (where coal and sandstone were once worked) and on to the ruins of Tefrane colliery [2]. Continue on the coast path overlooking St Brides Bay [3] to reach the minor road leading down to Newgale.

2. Turn right and continue uphill, passing Maidenhall car park on your right, to reach a T junction. Bear left and continue ahead – to the north stands Roch castle, guardian of the Landsker line since the 13th century, and now a private residence.

3. After a short distance bear right onto a signposted track which continues behind the remains of World War II bunkers to join a minor road. Continue ahead and downhill to rejoin the starting point.

FACILITIES

Seasonal public toilets at the car park by the Mariners Inn. Car park, shop and toilets at the Newgale end of the walk.

More walking books
by the author Paul Williams
and published by Gwasg Carreg Gwalch:

WALKS WITH HISTORY SERIES: CIRCULAR WALKS IN SOUTH PEMBROKESHIRE
£5.50

An informative guide to 14 selected circular walks varying in length and difficulty, which highlight south Pembrokeshire's outstanding landscape, beauty and history. Black-and-white route maps.

TEIFI & CARMARTHENSHIRE CIRCULAR WALKS
Paperback, 136 pages
£5.50

An interesting collection of 16 circular walks in Carmarthenshire and the Teifi valley (4-9.75 miles in length), comprising clear maps and detailed route notes, including valuable information about the archaeology and history, churches and castles and other points of interest. 27 black-and-white illustrations and 17 maps.